UNDERSTANDING
WILL SELF

Understanding Contemporary British Literature
Matthew J. Bruccoli, Series Editor

Volumes on

UNDERSTANDING
WILL SELF

M. Hunter Hayes

The University of South Carolina Press

© 2007 University of South Carolina

Published by the University of South Carolina Press
Columbia, South Carolina 29208

www.sc.edu/uscpress

Manufactured in the United States of America

16 15 14 13 12 11 10 09 08 07   10 9 8 7 6 5 4 3 2 1

Library of Congress Cataloging-in-Publication Data

Hayes, M. Hunter, 1965–
   Understanding Will Self / M. Hunter Hayes.
      p. cm.— (Understanding contemporary British literature)
   Includes bibliographical references and index.
   ISBN-13: 978-1-57003-675-0 (cloth : alk. paper)
   ISBN-10: 1-57003-675-6 (cloth : alk. paper)
   1. Self, Will—Criticism and interpretation. I. Title.
   PR6069.E3654Z68 2007
   823'.914—dc22

                                                      2006037505

For Sandy, Alex, and Sophie

Contents

Series Editor's Preface

The volumes of *Understanding Contemporary British Literature* have been planned as guides or companions for students as well as good nonacademic readers. The editor and publisher perceive a need for these volumes because much of the influential contemporary literature makes special demands. Uninitiated readers encounter difficulty in approaching works that depart from the traditional forms and techniques of prose and poetry. Literature relies on conventions, but the conventions keep evolving; new writers form their own conventions—which in time may become familiar. Put simply, *UCBL* provides instruction in how to read certain contemporary writers—identifying and explicating their material, themes, use of language, point of view, structures, symbolism, and responses to experience.

The word *understanding* in the titles was deliberately chosen. Many willing readers lack an adequate understanding of how contemporary literature works; that is, what the author is attempting to express and the means by which it is conveyed. Although the criticism and analysis in the series have been aimed at a level of general accessibility, these introductory volumes are meant to be applied in conjunction with the works they cover. They do not provide a substitute for the works and authors they introduce, but rather prepare the reader for more profitable literary experiences.

M. J. B.

Acknowledgments

Many institutions and people have provided me with generous assistance during the course of writing this book. I am grateful for various means of support given to me by the Department of Literature and Languages, Texas A&M University—Commerce, and the staff of Gee Library, also at Texas A&M University —Commerce. Among colleagues and individuals who have been unfailingly generous, I thank James Diedrick (Agnes Scott College), an invaluable source of information and friendship; Stephen Souris (Texas Woman's University), who invited me to speak on Self's work as part of the Professor's Corner series in Denton, Texas, during the writing of this book; Richard Todd (Leiden University), a wealth of knowledge on all aspects of British literature; Nicholas Burrows; and Martin Richardson. I also wish to express my gratitude to Will Self, who has generously assisted me with bibliographic queries, as well as making available to me several works including the typescript of *The Book of Dave* prior to its publication.

UNDERSTANDING
WILL SELF

CHAPTER ONE

Understanding Will Self

A full-time professional writer for more than fifteen years, Will Self quickly gained several distinctions, including seeing his name transformed into an adjective. Reviewers have branded his novels and short stories as "Selfian," a term employed both negatively and positively, as a way of describing his idiosyncratic style and fictional universe.[1] On the cover of the uncorrected proof of Self's third novel, *How the Dead Live,* appears what might be understood as his narrative raison d'être: "I don't write fiction for people to identify with and I don't write a picture of the world they can recognise. I write to astonish people."

The author of sixteen books to date—a body of work that comprises novels, short stories, nonfiction, and a comic strip—Self has maintained a consistently high public profile since the publication of *The Quantity Theory of Insanity* in 1991. Winner of the 1993 Geoffrey Faber Memorial Prize and shortlisted for the 1992 John Llewellyn Rhys Prize, his first short story collection brought him immediate recognition and carried enthusiastic comments by Martin Amis, J. G. Ballard, and other prominent novelists. This attention prompted the novelist Zoë Heller to proclaim in 1993 that "Self has probably won more praise—and praise of a more uninhibited kind—than any writer to emerge in the last decade."[2] Despite not yet having published a novel, Self was included in *Granta* magazine's 1993 list of the twenty "Best of Young British Novelists," leading Salman Rushdie to observe that Self was "already a cult figure."[3] Critical opinions on Self's writing remain divided. Acquiring endorsements from prominent literary critics including Harold Bloom while also being the target of others' critical ire, Self has continued to garner praise for his inventiveness and willingness to explore difficult issues in his writing. Typically set in and around the relatively compact geographical confines of metropolitan London, Self's fiction seldom lapses into parochialism and has been translated into several languages worldwide.

Self has also maintained a career as a journalist, writing at one time or another for each of the major newspapers in England and for many other publications in Britain and the United States. In addition to writing freelance reviews and essays, he has served as a restaurant critic, columnist, movie reviewer, social and political commentator, and as an analyst of nearly every other aspect of popular culture. Self's media presence extends to television and radio, and he has appeared regularly on BBC programs such as *Shooting Stars, Room 101, Have I Got News for You,* and *Grumpy Old Men,* as well as delivering the Saturday Essay for the BBC's Radio 4. In 2002 Self reported on Britain's prominence in international arms trading, serving as the BBC correspondent for a televised documentary.[4] Because of his various activities and high public profile, observers might infer that he not only runs the risk of media saturation but that he takes his audience for granted, a notion Self adamantly rejects. "To be allowed to write and to have an audience is always a privilege— never a right," he insists.[5]

Some critics have nominated Self as the presumptive heir to novelists such as Amis and Ballard; others have attempted to dismiss his work as the overrated product of a novelist who strives to shock his readers and whose subject matter and stylistic technique mark him as a writer too easily susceptible to excessive indulgences. One paradox of his work is that his settings are both recognizable and strange, and his prose style emphasizes this union's surrealist effects. He has been criticized for using arcane words and expressions, and a few reviewers have jokingly speculated that he keeps an inkhorn, or hoard of baroque words, on hand to dip into as necessary. Self has, however, been candid about the practicality of using a thesaurus. "To me, a writer saying he doesn't use one is like a mechanic saying he doesn't use a socket set," he told one interviewer.[6] His analogy risks a faulty comparison: Self's style is mechanical only in the sense that he lays bare the mechanisms involved in the creative process, including lexicality. He pairs seemingly incongruent concepts and levels of diction to create precise verbal juxtapositions.

When Self employs an unusual term, he is more fastidious than pretentious. John Walsh ignores this point when he writes that "not since the heyday of Anthony Burgess has there appeared an author so belligerently keen on strange words" and that the effect "is often to obscure rather than to illuminate."[7] Such opinions are common in the reviews of Self's books. Tom Shone detects a lexical similarity between Self's writing and the work of Amis and Ian McEwan, asserting in his review of *The Quantity Theory of Insanity* that Self's "language starts to resemble the standard-issue fingernail-paring prose typical of callow male writers."[8] John Keenan, however, peers beyond the surface of Self's prose to identify what it elucidates. "Like Celine," Keenan remarks, identifying one of the many writers to whose work Self's fiction is allied, "Self recognizes that the most effective way to depict the ugliness and stupidity of human behaviour is in prose of crystalline purity."[9] Self's "lexical palette"[10] serves to express an immediate comprehension of the various psychic and emotional states his characters experience.

This method draws the reader closer to the story—creating a paradox of fictional naturalism as Self often emphasizes what he views as an inherent failure of fiction to firmly establish grounds for the reader to suspend disbelief—by effectively making the reader complicit in the narrative process. But Self's technique cannot be reduced simply to his vocabulary, however impressive or annoying its range might appear to his readers. His prose style often leaps between journalistic declarative sentences and rapid verbal riffing, expanding the dimensions of his extended metaphors and descriptive catalogues.

The satirical abrasiveness of Self's fiction further exacerbates such diametric views. Some reviewers—emphasizing the florid descriptions of bodily secretions, the graphic depictions of violence, and the recurrent presence of psychotropic drugs in his work—regard Self as a puerile and frivolous writer. Others consider his use of these elements as resembling variously Jonathan Swift, Franz Kafka, and William Burroughs. Each of these comparisons holds merit. Self's work contains striking contradictions at times, demanding that readers believe in the veracity of his fictional world while intentionally undermining the very processes that would make such consideration possible. At once, Self can satirize social institutions, portray moments of pained introspection, and set out to tease the reader by testing the limits of narrative propriety. Despite such impishness there remains a cohesive seriousness to his work.

Self's fiction and nonfiction examine issues pertinent to contemporary society and to postwar literature. The anxieties of identity, most especially those concerning gender roles, sexuality, the autonomy of selfhood, and the pressure of social class, are present throughout his fiction and essays. Likewise his enduring scrutiny of the social, personal, and intellectual ramifications of clinical psychiatry, popular psychology, drugs, and the influence of the mass media invest his writing with a moral thrust. Despite their experimental and individualistic nature, Self's stories and novels frequently express conventional principles such as the longing for familial harmony and social acceptance. While his fiction is at times markedly self-reflexive, he avoids solipsism by delving into subjects of collective significance.

In his introduction to a reissue of *Alice's Adventures in Wonderland,* Self writes that since his childhood this book has held an enduring grip on his imagination. He credits it with providing him in nascent form vital themes that characterize his own work: "the text itself has always been with me, forming some of the fundamental antinomies that constitute my imagination: the juxtaposition of the quotidian and the fantastic; the transposition of irreconcilable elements; the distortion of scale as a means of renouncing the sensible in favour of the intelligible; and most importantly, abrupt transmogrification conceived of as integral to the human condition."[11] In his fiction Self insists that the readers maintain a suspension of disbelief to enter parallel worlds that can seem simultaneously alien and familiar, and Self's work often challenges the assumptions that underlie the illusion. This conveys an impression of surrealism, both in the broader sense of a "super realism" that extends beyond the limits of consciously perceived reality, and in the more specific Freudian-inspired sense that the French poet André Breton advocated in his second surrealist manifesto (1929) as a means of reconciling the unconscious (and semiconscious) mind with the conscious in order to gain new perspectives. The resulting surrealist and absurdist qualities that emerge from Self's juxtapositions with skillfully delineated quotidian details are best understood in Self's own description of his work as "dirty magical realism."[12]

While partly facetious, this phrase perfectly conveys his descriptive textures and narrative approach.

Self's name temptingly evokes that of John Self, the narrator of Martin Amis's 1984 novel, *Money,* and Amis has stated that he views Self as his successor.[13] Although Self has created his own niche as a writer, there are notable stylistic similarities between both novelists. "Like Amis," Self claims, "a part of my project has been to apply Mandarin language, the language of the intellectual classes, to demotic and popular culture subjects and conversely to apply demotic language and popular language to some of the concerns and ideas of the intellectual Mandarin classes. There's that kind of miscegenation, a kind of rubbing up against the traditional categories of English literary concern."[14] A significant characteristic of Self's narrative vision, this mingling of divergent "classes" has created part of his public persona as well. As Zoë Heller points out, Self's "curriculum vitae, combining as it does the tony (Oxford) with the boho (drugs), reads like a book publicist's wish list."[15]

The complexity of Self's public image, one that he has cultivated in part, is closely tied to his writing. His fiction and journalism convey a theatrical characteristic; the reader remains aware of the author as performer. Self's public readings reveal his dynamic flair for verbal ranges as he slips in and out of the various accents and speech patterns that distinguish his characters. He has also staged recitals of his short story "Scale" and has installed himself as a performance art exhibition in an art gallery, composing on a laptop computer his "live novella" and encouraging spectators to become direct participants in the creative act. In 2001 Self contributed a conceptual art installation titled *L'Ennui* for the 6th Lyon Biennale of Contemporary Art. Such activities remain secondary to his fiction, which for all its surreal and absurd elements remains more rooted in his own experiences than might initially seem apparent.

William Woodard Self was born in London on 26 September 1961. His parents, Elaine Rosenbloom Self and Peter Self, a publishing assistant and a political-science professor respectively, had separated temporarily prior to his birth, and, as Self has written, his mother planned to terminate her pregnancy until Anthony Storr, a prominent psychoanalyst who had been treating her for depression, advised her against doing so.[16] Although Self's parents remained married until his teenage years, the marriage was frequently one of mutual animosity. As Self's elder brother Jonathan writes in his memoir, *Self Abuse,* the family home was riven by the parents' domestic rows. In *Perfidious Man,* Will Self recounts of his parents' marriage that "it was not so much an open secret that theirs was an open marriage, as an open sore. An unutterably grey nimbus surrounded them, permeated from time to time by the lightning strikes of anger expressed by one or the other. I grew up in this cloud of knowingness, to become that most awful of things, a jaded innocent, and a promiscuous idealist."[17]

Self's formative years were spent in the north London suburb of East Finchley, though he occasionally lays claim to the adjacent Hampstead Garden Suburb. Although as a teenager he might have sought to escape north London, as a writer he has been drawn repeatedly to the area, "the sort of place that could grow a J. G. Ballard out of the mildest and least imaginative of psyches."[18] These suburbs retain a strong presence in his fiction; much of his work is set in north London, expressing a firm sense of place and scale. Self has long been interested in the interlocking relationships between place, identity, and cognition: the "psychogeography" that provides a virtual map to the topography of one's consciousness. London and its outlying environs lends Self's fiction a continuity that while not exactly linear manages to convey a sense of solidity and stability in the face of change. More than just a backdrop for most of his fiction, London functions as one of Self's most ambitious and recurring characters, one that appropriately seems to be both alien and familiar; it remains one of his most prevalent subjects and a demanding muse. Similarly Self's family life and childhood continue to influence his writing.

His mother arrived in England from upstate New York accompanied by her eleven-year-old son, Nicholas Adams, after discovering that she was three months pregnant following a brief affair with Peter Self when he was a visiting professor at Cornell University in 1958.[19] Educated at Pennsylvania State University, she placed tremendous value on literature and worked in publishing before and after her marriage to Peter Self: first in New York during the 1940s and '50s as a secretary to Harry Abrams at the Book-of-the-Month Club and at his own firm, and then in London during the 1970s and '80s at Duckworth, for whom she cowrote a book on cooking.[20] Prior to leaving the United States for England, she was married to Robert M. Adams, a prominent literary critic and scholar. According to Jonathan Self, literature formed a significant part of her self-identity:

> Books played a critical role at every juncture of my mother's life: they got her to university; they got her to work; and they helped her to attract the men that Grandma Lily had said would never be interested. More than this, they gave her status. This was particularly true when she came to England in the 1950s. She may have been an outsider—American, Jewish, divorced and from a poor background—but she was

exceptionally and undeniably well read. Faced with the crushing superiority and deep-rooted (if cleverly disguised) prejudices of the English upper classes, my mother's understanding of literature helped not only to save her from overwhelming feelings of inadequacy and inferiority but also to help win friends.[21]

Because, perhaps, her life was filled with anxiety, upheaval, and disappointment, literature offered Elaine Self a comforting consolation. At home, family dinners regularly became an event of her own design, the "Reading Supper," where she and her two sons by Peter Self would eat and read in silence. Just as the deceased mother in "The North London Book of the Dead" is first glimpsed strolling through Crouch End while carrying a Barnes & Noble book bag, suggesting that books are a part of her afterlife routine, Self's mother shared the habit: "To ensure that her bookishness did not go unnoticed, my mother made a great display of her love of the printed word. She carried a canvas bag with her wherever she went; she haunted little-known libraries; and she carefully arranged piles of seemingly haphazardly stacked books at strategic points around the house. As a consequence of their importance in her life, books became sacred items, to be worshipped and revered."[22]

Possessing a "hair-trigger temper and phobic anxieties,"[23] Elaine Self was given to sudden mood swings—a "whim of iron"[24]—and became a domineering presence at home. "Her rule was absolute and she enforced it through a combination of fear, physical force, disapproval and sarcasm," Jonathan Self recalls. "Yet what really enabled her to achieve her psychic invasion of my brothers and me was something entirely different: her vulnerability. My mother needed us. She hurt, and her anguish bound us to her."[25] She has continued to be a formidable and prominent influence on her youngest son's life and fiction. Her death from lung cancer in 1988 gave him the subject for "The North London Book of the Dead," which appears in *The Quantity Theory of Insanity,* and *How the Dead Live.* Self began writing in earnest after her death, and one possible factor for this burst of creative energy is a combination of grief and a sense of relief at no longer having to worry about obtaining her approval or scorn with his literary endeavors.

Will Self's father's family contrasts significantly with his mother's background. Peter Self came from a family of modest privilege and intellectual recognition. His ancestors include prominent members and pastors of the Church of England, as well as the founder of Lancing College, Nathaniel Woodard. Educated at Lancing and Oxford, Peter Self wrote several books on urban planning and political economics, and he held several prominent academic appointments, including positions at the London School of Economics and Political Science, the University of London, and the Australian National University, Canberra. Whereas Elaine Self could be aggressive, Peter Self frequently appeared aloof, impatient, and insensitive to his children, "a man who uses dialectics the way the Japanese used bamboo slivers during the war,"[26] as well as graceless and socially awkward. Because both of his parents had previous marriages, Self has said that "my childhood was their second act."[27] His cousin Susannah Self, an internationally acclaimed composer and mezzo-soprano, once remarked that his parents "absolutely adored him. There was a sense that the one thing that held together their difficult marriage was their total adoration of their little Willy. Day in, day out, they had nothing but pathological wonder for their incredibly naughty and difficult creation."[28] Jonathan Self provides one further explanation for his parents' preference of their youngest son over his elder brother and half brother. "From an early age it was clear that my younger brother possessed the very thing which our parents set the greatest store by: an exceptionally brilliant mind."[29]

These two sources of familial identity—Jewish-American on one side, Anglican on the other, both caustic intellectuals—have given Will Self the basis for much of his fiction. He has plumbed his parents' psyches and his own experiences in order to create many of his fictional characters, and he drew directly from his mother's diaries and loosely from her life when writing *How the Dead Live* from the perspective of Lily Bloom. But as an adolescent he had begun already to include parts of his mother's personality into his own, particularly involving the hostility from his parents' dissolving marriage. In *Perfidious Man,* Self recalls his mother's verbal affronts directed at his father. "She ridiculed the way he spoke, walked[,] acted and thought. Everything about him was—she implied—fit for murder. She taught us to loathe him as she did, and in the way that she did. I grew to biological manhood with the body of a frustrated, depressed, middle-aged woman, not so much trapped—as hiding inside me."[30] Aspects of both parents appear in *My Idea of Fun,* among other works. As this novel's narrator, Ian Wharton, describes his domineering mother he suggests that "she must have seen something in Wharton senior, some potential. Clearly he was from a better class and perhaps that was sufficient. Mum is an expert, like so many English people, not only at detecting class origins in others, but also at obscuring her own."[31] As Nick Rennison points out, Self "is sometimes presented as a bad-boy outsider, writing, like the Americans Williams Burroughs or Hubert Selby Jnr, about sex, drugs and violence in a very direct way. Yet he is not some class warrior storming the citadels of the literary establishment from the outside but an Oxford-educated, middle-class metropolitan who, despite his protestations to the contrary in interviews, is about as much at the heart of that establishment as you can get, a place he has occupied almost from the start of his career."[32]

Drugs and psychiatry form two persistent subjects in Self's fiction. There is a widespread presumption that Self glamorizes drug use in his writing, but almost all accounts of narcotics and other drugs in his fiction point toward the trauma of addiction. By his own admission, Self began smoking marijuana daily when he was twelve years old, quickly escalating to harder drugs: "I started taking drugs on a daily basis when I was 5 ft. 4 in. and stopped when I was 6 ft. 4 in. A foot of narcosis."[33] When he was fourteen he began frequenting the local pubs in Finchley. At seventeen he began injecting heroin, and within three years he had become an addict and—like Ian Wharton in *My Idea of Fun* —had been diagnosed as a "borderline personality."[34] Initially, his brother writes, the idea of Self's experimenting with drugs appealed to their mother's bohemian sense of rebellion: "Far from discouraging Will's passion for drugs, my mother had actively promoted it. While he was still at school she propagated marijuana for his use—deriving considerable amusement from the thought that she was engaging in an illegal activity. Later, when he was at university, she had given him extra money to support his habit. . . . As Will's behaviour became increasingly disturbed she acknowledged her mistake."[35]

A precocious intellectual, Self read vociferously throughout his youth and justified his drug use to conform to the popular Beat image of writers such as William Burroughs, whom Self began reading during his teens. As at home, with his parents' laissez-faire attitudes toward childrearing, at Christ's College, the local grammar school in Finchley that he attended after progressing through Golders Hill primary school in Barnet and then University College Junior School in Hampstead, Self had little against which he could rebel. Two teachers at Christ's College encouraged his writing and intellectual development, and the school emerges in his fiction as Markhams College in "Bull," as Ian Wharton's alma mater Varndean Grammar in *My Idea of Fun,* and as Creighton Comprehensive in his short story "The Indian Mutiny."[36]

Self entered Oxford in 1979, studying politics, philosophy, and economics (PPE) at Exeter College. Because Self read philosophy rather than English literature, some reviewers of his work have suggested that he possesses an inferiority complex as a novelist which manifests itself in his exuberant writing style. John Walsh, for example, has said that Self "would rather use the word terpsichorean than the word dancing. His problem is that he went to Martin Amis's—and also my—college in Oxford: Exeter. But he studied PPE by mistake. Now he's trying to write a series of Eng Lit essays, 'Is this good enough? Damn it, I should have done English!'"[37] While variations of Walsh's sentiment appear in other articles about Self, they are speciously reductive, failing to consider the significance philosophy holds in his writing and the verbal effects his prose style generates. Self has a complex set of literary touchstones and sources of inspiration if not direct influence. Although contemporary British novelists such as Amis, Ballard, and Alasdair Gray certainly inform portions of Self's work, tones of other writers including Fyodor Dostoevsky, Nikolai Gogol, Franz Kafka, Georges Simenon, and the Americans Woody Allen and Joseph Heller resonate in his fiction.

At Oxford, Self devoted more energy to extracurricular activities than to his studies. During his so-called anarchistic phase, he fronted a band called the Abusers. Drugs became central to

Self's life, assuming a greater importance than his studies. According to Tom Shone, Self "went to one lecture in his entire university career, wrote frazzled but dazzling philosophy essays in his spare time, and spent most of the rest of it exploring Oxford's drug demi-monde of boho low-lifes and downwardly mobile aristocrats."[38] As he was about to sit his final exams, Self was arrested for drug possession and faced the ominous prospect of prosecution. Although he graduated from Oxford in 1982, he received a Third, partly a result of the pending court case during his exams. This precluded him from returning to pursue postgraduate studies.[39]

Self has stated that his immersion in the drug community introduced him to this peculiar social mélange and the language that arises from it, but it took him years to work these onto the page even though he was writing fiction during this period. Not surprisingly, rather than advancing his talent, his drug use actually stymied its development. As he told London's *Sunday Times Magazine,* "The abyss between my aspirations and what was appearing on the paper was so hideously large that I can relate almost every aspect of my aberrant behaviour at that point to my thwarted writing ambitions."[40]

After leaving Oxford with his M.A., he fell into a variety of odd jobs, working as a laborer, a road sweeper on the A101, running a playground, and serving a stint in Australia for the Darwin Land Commission. This period constitutes one of Self's own gray areas, with his desire to be a writer running into conflict with his inability to produce publishable fiction. As a compensation of sorts, in the mid-1980s Self began publishing his cartoons in *City Lights* and the *New Statesman.* The eponymous character in *Slump,* his strip in the *New Statesman,* exemplifies elements of Self's life. Slump lives on the dole—his name embodies economic depression as well as his own indolence—and decides to absent himself from the external world by refusing to leave his bed. In one late installment, Slump imagines that he has died in bed and that no one finds his corpse for several months, leaving his duvet covered in a "putrescent green slime"; the punch line, "as in life . . . so in death,"[41] provides an early occurrence of the dominant motif in "The North London Book of the Dead," presenting life and death as similar states of existence. *Slump* is at once an extended rant on indolence and an ironic expression of Self's own anxieties during this period. The strip ran regularly for two years, until Self was fired because the strip was deemed to be "too depressing," and it was collected in a volume brought out by Virgin in 1985. Although *Slump* has long been out of print, Self has published other drawings in his nonfiction collections *Junk Mail* and *Sore Sites*.

At his mother's expense, in 1986 Self sought treatment for alcohol and drug dependency. He draws from his experiences at the rehabilitation clinic at Weston-super-Mare in *The Quantity Theory of Insanity.* Zack Busner's Concept House and Ward 9 of Heath Hospital seem to particularly fictionalize this period of his life. Self abstained from drugs and alcohol for more than three years, relapsing in 1989 after Bloomsbury accepted his manuscript of *The Quantity Theory of Insanity.* In between he worked for a corporate publisher, and then in the late 1980s he wrote a column called "Malespeak" for *She* magazine, and he continues to work in journalism.

Self married Kate Chancellor in June 1989, a year after his mother's death and shortly before Bloomsbury decided to publish *The Quantity Theory of Insanity.* Their son, Alexis, was born in 1990, and their daughter, Madeleine, was born in 1992. Self and his wife separated in 1993, formally dissolving their marriage three years later. In 1997 he married the journalist Deborah Orr, with whom he has two sons, Ivan (born 1997) and Luther (born 2001).

Self has repeatedly termed the 1990s a period of decadence, a fin de siécle reminiscent of the 1890s. It is a decadence that he understands from personal experience as well as objective observation. He is infamous for having snorted heroin on board John Major's jet while covering the general election for the *Observer* in April 1997. Self was dismissed from the paper and for several days the episode played out in the news section of the tabloids and major papers, an experience to which he alludes in the title of his second collection of essays and reviews, *Feeding Frenzy.* The imbroglio marks one of his lowest points with drug and alcohol abuse, prompting him once again to seek treatment. Consistently sober for the first time in several years, and after missing several deadlines, Self published *How the Dead Live* in 2000.

The novel has been regarded as his most successful work to date. It is also his most personal. Adopting many of the concepts from the *Tibetan Book of the Dead,* the novel elaborates on themes in "The North London Book of the Dead," this time using a character based on his mother as the narrator. Lily Bloom, like Elaine Self, is a Jewish-American expatriate who dies at age sixty-five. Self used his mother's diaries for many of Lily's expressions in the novel, and he examines his addictions through Lily's youngest daughter, the junkie Natasha. After writing two-thirds of a screenplay for a cinema adaptation of Oscar Wilde's *The Picture of Dorian Gray,* Self was unable to reach a satisfying ending and produced instead his fourth novel, *Dorian: An Imitation* (2002). In this novel he examines contemporary society and the art milieu from the advent of AIDS in the 1980s to the death of Princess Diana, ascribing to this new decadent period a stringent narcissism and banalization of feeling that gives new evidence for what J. G. Ballard has termed "the death of affect."[42] As Henry Wotton informs Baz Hallward in Self's *Dorian,* "Who gives a shit about being too decadent, when to be contemporary is to be absolutely so?"[43] With *The Book of Dave* (2006), Self divides his narrative between the recent past and distant future in order to express fundamental concerns about religious fervor, masculine identity, and familial harmony and discord.

Although Self is best known for his novels, critics often devalue them while writing admiringly about his short stories. Because Self has throughout his first several books shown a marked preference for exploring ideas rather than developing the psychological verisimilitude typically associated with characterization, his approach tests the patience of some readers when extended for hundreds of pages. With its sustained barrage of verbal irony, parataxis (sentences with clauses linked by coordination rather than subordination), and oscillating diction, his prose style finds in the focus that the shorter form entails a symbiosis between technique, narrative pacing, expository development, and other formal components. His stories exploit the condensed form to provide an intense concentration of linguistic play and frequently absurdist imagery, and the compact structure of the shorter form complements the exuberance of his narrative technique. Devoted to exposing what he sees as the excessive indulgences and the stilting banality of much of modern society, Self creates in his short stories cross-sections of contemporary urban life, providing satirically revealing dissections of a decadent society.

While he is frequently compared to Jonathan Swift because of the prevalence of satire, Self distances himself from the moral pontifications traditionally found in the form. He has argued that "the new problem that satirists have to face is moral relativism. And in that context, it seems to me that the role of satire that I produce is to make the audience think for themselves. It is to throw the whole burden of moral thought back on the audience. So I am not trying to convert people to anything but thinking seriously. I'm trying to be a provocateur."[44] His short fiction encapsulates many of the motifs that he develops further in his longer works.

The majority of Self's stories have been collected in *The Quantity Theory of Insanity; Grey Area; Tough, Tough Toys for Tough, Tough Boys;* and *Dr Mukti and Other Tales of Woe.* Although many of Self's stories stand apart from the rest of his oeuvre, certain key works link directly to other short stories and his novels to form a body of self-referential narratives. Familiar characters, ideas, locations, and themes permeate Self's fictional world. Psychiatry, contemporary art and its milieu, and the media as subjects for satire dominate his fiction. His short stories introduce readers to these themes and to characters that typify them, positing crucial details that resurface in subsequent stories and novels. Moreover their arrangement in his collections provides a key to ascertaining their importance in the vast linked narrative his works constitute. Like Marcel Proust's *A la recherché du temps perdu,* commonly translated into English as *Remembrance of Things Past,* and Anthony Powell's *Dance to the Music of Time, a* twelve-volume novel sequence, Self's body of work can be seen as a *roman-fleuve,* a set of independent yet interrelated fictional works with reappearing characters. In a discussion of his views on literary realism, Self addresses his conception of this cohesive narrative and the point it serves, a method that he initially devised as a way of arranging the stories in *The Quantity Theory of Insanity*:

> In my first collection of short stories characters from one narrative would reappear in others, either taking up a minor role, or even merely as a subject of hearsay, or seen—in passing— on television. This, I hoped, would help my readers to understand that the world of my books had an autonomous and believable existence. It's a method that I still adhere to, every one of my books has a series of links to at least one of my other works, and by extension to the whole oeuvre. Does it matter to anyone save for me? I have no idea, but that itself doesn't matter, the important thing is that I am able to suspend disbelief in my own creations, because if I don't—who will?[45]

Similarly there are frequent overlaps between Self's fiction and his journalism, and together these help readers in understanding both the similarities and differences between Self's fictional world and his actual environment.

Self has collected a considerable amount of his nonfiction in three key works: *Junk Mail* (1995), *Sore Sites* (2000), and *Feeding Frenzy* (2001), along with his essay in *Perfidious Man* (2000) and his introductions to books by various writers and artists. His journalism ranges from ephemeral commentary to serious examinations of contemporary social and political issues, and Self's comments on literature and contemporary art particularly help to bring into focus the various attitudes and preoccupations that typify the current zeitgeist.

Even though a collection such as *Feeding Frenzy* provides a fair sample of the diversity of Self's journalism—including essays and reviews of books, films, television programs, and restaurants—it must exclude much more, thereby giving an inadequate perception of how much he has published. "Writing," he observed presciently early in his career, "can be a kind of addiction too, you know."[46]

CHAPTER TWO

Urban Bedlam
The Quantity Theory of Insanity

Will Self and *The Quantity Theory of Insanity* entered London's literary world with generous endorsements. Published as a paperback original in Britain, followed two years later by a hardcover edition in the United Kingdom and five years later in the United States, the book featured blurbs by Martin Amis, Beryl Bainbridge, and Doris Lessing.[1] Amis also nominated the collection as one of his favorite books of the year, noting its "originality" and "sheer braininess."[2] Readers were introduced to a newcomer who brought with him the approval of major postwar writers. As a literary debut, *The Quantity Theory of Insanity* seems uncharacteristic, eschewing the conventional bildungsroman and other egoistic tendencies typical of an apprentice work. None of the stories appeared in print prior to the book's publication, and the book as a whole imparts an impression of a fractured novel.

Individual stories are carefully arranged to reveal submerged details gradually. The two works that frame the collection, "The North London Book of the Dead" and "Waiting," superficially appear to have little in common other than Self's ability to transform London geography into a metaphorical emblem of psychic deracination. However, these stories depict a city in which apparently chance encounters suggest that coincidences might in fact be products of an unseen control. Still one of Self's most celebrated stories, "The North London Book of the Dead" introduces these motifs through its depiction of grief. In keeping with the majority of his early fiction, it presents a first-person narrative that plays on confessional impulses.

Like Gogol and Kafka, Self blends commonplace descriptions and extraordinary events in an even, objective tone. The unnamed narrator begins with an admission of uncertainty and a desire to see his situation as typical, noting that "I suppose the form my bereavement took after my mother died was fairly conventional. Initially I was shocked."[3] Alluding to Marcel Proust's *Swann's Way*, the narrator remarks that "like Marcel after Albertine has gone, from time to time I felt that the reason I no longer missed Mother with such poignancy was that I had become another person. I had changed. I was no longer the sort of person who had a mother like Mother" (5). This epiphanic moment, however, is obliterated during a chance outing in a London suburb.

As he walks "down Crouch Hill towards Crouch End on a drizzly, bleak, Tuesday afternoon" (5) he sees his mother across the road. Rather than draw attention to the fantastic elements of this vision, Self instead emphasizes minute details: "She was wearing a sort of bluish, tweedish long jacket and black slacks and carrying a Barnes & Noble book bag, as well as a large handbag and a carrier bag from Waitrose. She had a CND badge in her lapel and was observing the world with a familiar 'there will be tears before bedtime' sort of expression" (5). These particulars establish the authority of the narrator's image of his mother, one that closely replicates the description of his mother from recurring images of seeing women who resembled her (4). This juxtaposition of phantom mothers and the real one poses two questions: whether he had in fact been seeing his mother during previous outings or whether the latest vision was a more pronounced false illusion.

The subtle expression of the mother's personality through the Campaign for Nuclear Disarmament badge she wears merits attention. In "Waiting," the story that closes *The Quantity Theory of Insanity,* a central character, Jim Stonehouse, faces prosecution for a hit-and-run traffic accident. The victim, Takis Christos, is a Greek Cypriot produce merchant and a Crouch End resident. After testifying, he joins his companions in the courtroom: "They were a couple of sharpish young men who looked like estate agents; and a plump woman in late middle age wearing elephantine slacks and a CND sticker on her raincoat" (208). To make the link between these two stories clear to attentive readers, Self gives Christos the same address, 24 Rosemount Avenue, as the narrator's mother in "The North London Book of the Dead." Additionally, Christos is explicitly mentioned in the opening story, where the mother states that "he's a friend of mine—a Greek Cypriot—he runs a wholesale fruit business, but he writes in his spare time" (14). Christos, whose name translates from the Greek as "all holy Christ," serves as a secular messiah for the narrator's deceased mother, reinforcing the governing trope of a mundane paradise in suburban London. In *How the Dead Live*, Phar Lap Jones and a Cypriot taxi driver perform similar services for Lily Bloom. Stonehouse also appears in "Ward 9," where he occupies his time in a psychiatric ward—after the magistrate places him in the care of Dr. Zack Busner for psychological evaluation and possible treatment—by sculpting a model replica of the Marleybone Flyover complete with a traffic accident between two cars and "a small Japanese fruiterer's van which was coming in from the Edgware Road" (43). "Waiting" not only grants these characters—and others, including Busner —an encore; it further presses the conceit that the quick and the dead interact frequently without the living ever suspecting anything bizarre might be occurring.

Unlike its titular referents, the *Tibetan Book of the Dead* and the *Egyptian Book of the Dead,* the "North London Book of the Dead" does not serve as a manual to guide through the afterlife but is simply a postmortem telephone directory. The dead continue much as they had during their previous existence: "When you die you move to another part of London, that's all there is to it," the narrator's mother informs him (8). Self has acknowledged the influence of Martin Amis on his work, and in this story and its later incarnation, *How the Dead Live* (2000), he covers much of the same thematic terrain Amis did in *Other People: A Mystery Story* (1981), a novel whose dominant conceit is that death might be indistinguishable from life. Both writers satirize ontological and existentialist traditions as a means of drawing attention to states of estrangement in the contemporary city. Yet where Amis suspends recognition of his urban milieu, Self makes his London topography clearly recognizable.

Comparing the London of his fiction to Amis's descriptions of the capital, Self has commented on their divergent perceptions of the city, remarking that "My London is, I think, much more literal. . . . I can draw an A–Z of my London."[4] This literality becomes an expression for what Self identifies as his concern "with the physical reality of the buildings, the landscape."[5] The city emerges as a living organism—at times as a vital organ, a heart connected to a network of motorway arteries—that stands in vivid contrast to its existentially ambiguous inhabitants. As Philip Tew remarks, "Self's stories and novels reconsider alternate views of the contemporary city, a meta-reality of the return of the self, an afterlife in the current world, and the minutiae of the illusions of contemporary urban culture and its myths."[6] Self's overarching conceit in the story is that the dead and the living are indistinguishable, a trenchant satirical comment on the condition of metropolitan life. In the 1950s Peter Self addressed the issue of urban sprawl and its consequences, noting the ways in which the major high-density metropolitan "conurbations" encroach upon the countryside to form surrounding "twilight zones."[7] In "The North London Book of the Dead," Will Self invests this phrase with fresh meaning by creating an alternative London that upsets traditional metaphysical belief systems.

The story provides an appropriate introduction to Self's career by compounding many of the themes that he develops in later works: parental influence, geography's effects on identity and psychological bearing, and the creation of a fictional milieu that paradoxically seems both comfortably familiar and disturbingly alien. Just as the suburbs compel questions regarding the vitality and health of their occupants in the opening story, they also provide Self with a geographical epicenter of psychosis, a condition featured throughout the author's journalism and fiction.

Reviewing *The Quantity Theory of Insanity* for the *Times Literary Supplement* (*TLS*), Nick Hornby observes that "these stories are best read as feature articles about a parallel planet full of dreary but threatening institutions and extraordinary ideas."[8] Hornby identifies a key feature of Self's fictional universe: although it closely resembles the actual world, at times disturbingly so, its familiarity can be elusive. In accord with Self's attention to abrupt protean shifts, just as his fictional world seems recognizable it acquires new, typically menacing, aspects. By utilizing a small cast of recurring characters in this fictionalized landscape, Self establishes a sense of narrative distance that lends focus and a semblance of objectivity to his satirical attacks on what he sees as prominent ills in society.

Self's vision of contemporary society is one of decadence, forging a link between his work and that of writers from a century earlier, most prominently Oscar Wilde, Joris-Karl Huysmans, and Octave Mirbeau, as well as the Symbolist poet Charles Baudelaire. While both Wilde's *The Picture of Dorian Gray* (1891) and Huysmans's *À rebours* (1884) stand as exemplary decadent novels, they are also important precursors for Self's fiction. As the term denotes, "decadence" suggests a sense of decay or degeneration of moral, physical, and sensory customs; it also expresses temporal concern at the end of an era, commonly expressed as the fin de siècle. Although Self does not straightforwardly present the artist or aesthete as a privileged member of society, one liberated from moral judgment as Wilde advocates in his adoption of the Oxford critic Walter Pater's art-for-art's-sake maxim, he shares these writers' view of a degenerating society and an awareness of nihilism.

Two aspects of his perception of social decay are the exaggerated ethical breaches in psychiatry and academia, both of which typify the intelligentsia of his alternate universe. In "Ward 9," Self introduces Dr. Zachary Busner, a pop psychiatrist who emerges progressively in Self's subsequent stories and novels to become a leading character in his fiction. One reason Zack Busner emerges as such an important character in Self's fiction is that Busner is able to seize some semblance of control over the other characters, functioning as an interior counterpart to Self's exterior stage-managing of the scenes and events. In addition Busner enjoys fostering his image as a public celebrity.

Initially one of a group of promising graduate students who studied under a therapist and academic celebrity identified only as Alkan—the originator of an analytic method called Implication, to which he subjected his own students—Busner rejects conventional treatments. As Harold Ford, the narrator of "The Quantity Theory of Insanity" reveals, "Disgusted by his experience of hospital psychology—and the narrow drive to reduce mental illness to a chemical formula—Busner had rebelled" (119). Busner's unorthodox practices include an ill-fated attempt in the early 1970s to blur the distinctions between patients and doctors at his Concept House, a psycho-utopia that serves as an empathetic forerunner of the clinical methods employed in "Ward 9." The theoretical underpinning of his experiment suggests a post-structuralist approach to psychiatry, drawing attention to the inherent instability and indeterminacy of meaning that post-structuralism explores in linguistics: "It was dawning on me that whole way in which people have hitherto viewed mental illness has been philosophically suspect. The division between doctor and patient has corresponded to an unwarranted epistemological assumption" (119). As Busner is introduced, all of this lies in his past. He has achieved wealth and celebrity status through his invention of The Riddle, "a pop psychological device" (25) of ambiguous purpose or value that seems to have enjoyed the popularity of the Rubik's Cube, and through his frequent appearances on television and radio programs. Busner's ambition for fame and wealth, however, leads to questionable practices that will eventually propel him into criminal acts of escalating magnitude.

A nominal homage to "Ward No. 6" by Anton Chekhov, "Ward 9" is set in an isolated wing of Heath Hospital, where Busner works as "the senior consultant in the psychiatric department" (24). Although the story takes place following Busner's descent into madness after the collapse of his Concept House in Willesden, his drive for an empathetic symbiosis between therapist and patient remains intact, if more ominous than previously. On Ward 9 patients and therapists exist in arbitrarily prescribed roles; each has the freedom to decide which role to adopt. However, freedom in Self's fiction tends to be qualified, a point the critic Thomas Mallon makes when he calls Will Self "the most misnamed novelist of our time" because "his books show neither a belief in the first nor a permanent sense of the second."[9] Busner's utopian ideals devolve into a nightmarish dystopian scenario, and there exists the distinct possibility that this might be a continuation of the practical jokes Busner enjoyed playing on his colleagues as a graduate student under Alkan.

As with the preponderance of Self's early short stories, "Ward 9" features a first-person narrator. This point of view draws attention to the act of narration while also building an illusion of personal confession. By limiting the perspective to the protagonist's consciousness, Self places his narrator's ego and its attendant biases at the center of his narrative performance. The narrator of "Ward 9," Misha Gurney, recounts his entrapment in the hellish world of Busner's design after accepting a position as an art therapist on the ward. Misha's father, Simon, had been one of Alkan's promising students along with Busner before abandoning psychiatry to become a sculptor. This places Busner in a paternal role to Misha, but for Misha their relationship carries an enormous amount of psychological baggage:

Busner is the Hierophant.[10] He oversees the auguries, decocts potions, presides over rituals that piddle the everyday into a teastrainer reality. And he is a reminder of everything I wish to bury with my childhood. A world of complacency, of theory in the face of real distress. My father and Busner would sit together for hours at the head of the dining-room table and set the world to rights. Their conversation—I realised later—loaded with the slop of banality and sentimentality that was the direct result of their own sense of failure. Their wives would repair to another room and there do things that *had* to be done, while they carried on and on, eliding their adolescence still further into middle age. The awful oatmeal carpets of my childhood and the shame of having been a part of it all. When I think of Busner now he is a ghastly throwback, threatening to drag me into a conspiracy to evade reality. (57–58)

In a passage where Misha expresses a sense of anxiety stemming from Busner's continued absence from the ward, he implies that Busner had sexually molested him years previously: "I kept expecting the door to the utilities cupboard to swing open and to find him crouching there, sweaty pills in pudgy palm, the discredited guru, waiting with affectionate arm to jerk me off for old times' sake" (58). The psychiatric wards at Heath Hospital embody a failed sense of familial obligation and compassion.

Two patients on Ward 8, where they had been "farmed out" (61) to avoid disturbing Misha by their presence, include Mark Busner and Gerry Bowen, the latter of whom was Misha's predecessor and is the brother of Jane Bowen, the senior registrar for the psychiatric wards and an expert on eating disorders. Simon, a patient who is admitted to Ward 9 on a regular basis, is the son of a woman who holds a teaching appointment on the ward (52). Tom, a patient on the ward due to his "voluntary committal" (20), is the brother of Dr. Anthony Valuam. "We are all family," Busner tells Misha, pointing out that he has "come home to us" (66). "You see," Busner explains, "what we have here is a situation that calls for mutual aid. My son, Jane and Anthony's siblings, Simon, Jim, Clive, Harriet, indeed all of the patients on the ward, could be said to be casualties of a war that we ourselves have waged. That's why we felt it was our duty to care for them in a special kind of environment" (67). In this extended, "meta-mad" clan, three of whom factor significantly into several of Self's other works, Busner assumes the role of exacting patriarch, taking full control of his family.

Even Misha, whose first-person narration would seem to imply some autonomy, cannot escape Busner's machinations. Misha is given daily doses of Parstelin, a psychotropic drug that renders him aloof from caring about others or about anything—the mirror opposite of the experimental drug Inclusion in *Grey Area*. This psychological and emotional detachment from his environment develops into an abnegation of the moral authority Misha holds. The moral center of the story and ward alike, Misha becomes effectively neutered. His decline is represented by the fate of the "idiot" he encounters in the heath outside the hospital, a pathetic man who functions as a barometer of Misha's psychic state. As he encounters the idiot's corpse one morning, Misha observes that the Parstelin contains a "positive attribute," granting him "another fuzzy frame of reference, within which the idiot's death is no responsibility of mine. Someone else will report it, someone else will find him" (59). In addition Misha conducts a series of sexual encounters with a nurse, Mimi, who gives him the Parstelin, thus failing a test Busner has instigated. Busner informs Misha that "this is not the behaviour of a responsible therapist. You had a choice, Misha. On Ward 9 you could have been a therapist or patient; it seems that you have decided to become a patient" (67). But Busner is being disingenuous. As Mallon points out, Self's characters enjoy little free will; Misha Gurney responds as Busner—whose adult life has been spent studying human behavior—would have known all along.

Busner's failed Concept House and Ward 9 appear to have their actual origins in the rehabilitation center at Weston-super-Mare where Self was admitted in 1986 to free himself from heroin addiction. Although Concept House derives in part from R. D. Laing's Kingley Hall, in his fiction Self draws unmistakable correlations with drugs, addiction, illness, and madness, mining this vein of experience that had been a part of his life since he was twelve. Throughout Self's stories and novels, many of his seemingly most far-fetched conceits and details spring from his own trauma.[11]

In the collection's eponymous story, Harold Ford, the narrator and originator of the Quantity Theory of Insanity, sees a variation on Heisenberg's famous uncertainty principle in quantum mechanics at play in human social interaction where "the effect of observation has a direct impact on the nature of the event" (97). This story ostensibly clarifies Ford's career-making theory where there exists only a "fixed proportion of sanity available in any given society at any given time" (126). Aberrant behavior, then, is understood as the inevitable consequence of an exhausted distribution of sanity: thus the "surface of the collective psyche was like the worn, stripy ticking of an old mattress. If you punched into its coiled hide at any point, another part would spring up—there was no action without reaction, no laughter without tears, no normality without its pissing accompanist" (127). A convoluted pastiche of Jungian and chaos theories, Ford's breakthrough concept ushers in the so-called Quantity Age (142)—a period that coincides with the rise of post-structuralism and other theoretical underpinnings of postmodernism, an amorphous system of knowledge and artistic representation centering on relativism—and elevates him to the dubious position of the most orthodox of Alkan's students/analysands. The Quantity Theory, Ford writes as he recounts its and his twinned histories, moves quickly out of its academic origins to assume popular status as a nebulous entity resembling a cult, political ideology, and religion (134). "Even if the exact substance of the theory is difficult to define," Ford states, "it's quite easy to see why the theory appealed to people so strongly. It took that most hallowed of popular places, the within-the-walnut-shell-world of the mind, and stated that what went on inside it was effectively a function of mathematically observable fluctuations across given population groups. You no longer had to go in for difficult and painful therapies in order to palliate your expensive neuroses. Salvation was a matter of social planning" (134). Insisting that in identifying this revolutionary theory, one that compels a reconsideration of ontological and epistemological traditions, he "was merely describing, not prescribing" (134), Ford seeks to distance himself from his colleagues at Chelmsford. In the process the reader is given the back story of Alkan's former protégées, including Busner.

Initially an outsider to Alkan's swaggering elite researchers, Ford had long viewed them with suspicion, and he comments that "Alkan's bloods delighted in playing elaborate psychological tricks on one another—the aim of which was to convince the victim that he was psychotic" (102), a revelation that explains much of Busner's manipulations in "Ward 9," "Inclusion®," *Great Apes,* and "Dr Mukti." Referring to the men who would come to constitute the Quantity Theory research group, Ford avers that he "was so pleased to be accepted by them that I suppose the dawning awareness that I might in fact be their intellectual superior was enough to make me want to stick close" (124). Only Simon Gurney, who abandons psychiatry for art, establishes something resembling a friendship with Ford as each member of Alkan's elite attains a position of professional prominence. Adam Harley puts the theory into practice with his Exclusionist Therapy Movement (139) and ultimately accepts a position as Sanity Quotient Adviser to a large corporation (143); Phillip Hurst heads a new government bureau that attempts to establish "a sanity quotient of the whole country" (139); and Adam Sikorski effects a political response with his Situationist-like team of Radical Psychic Field Disruptionists (146). Alkan himself had previously gone completely insane, a fact Ford discovers after tracing his whereabouts in London by interpreting samples of random, subliterate sex graffiti in public toilets and establishing from them a synchronistic sequence of integers and geographical coordinates. As Alkan's former students assemble in Denver to attend a conference on the Quantity Theory, Ford's narrative dissolves as he speculates about the social consequences of mental illness becoming increasingly "concentrated around educational institutions" (149). This emphasizes Self's satirical comment on academia, which he ridicules through its own linguistic and semiotic traits.

In a tradition of writers that includes Jorge Luis Borges, Vladimir Nabokov, and David Lodge, Self burlesques scholarly prose. Academia is a favorite target for Self, suggesting not only his father's career but an awareness of how his own work might be analyzed. He has joked about his role as a critical subject, asserting that "I've always relished the idea of my work being not simply misunderstood by ordinary readers, but also comprehensively misinterpreted by the professionals."[12] Although "The Quantity Theory of Insanity" begins by resembling a personal report headed by a dateline, it adopts aspects of a scholarly article, becoming the definitive account of the theory's origins complete with the curriculum vitae of its principal figures.

Like J. G. Ballard, whose *Atrocity Exhibition* includes pseudoscientific papers, Self subverts the academic argot he assumes. The story and collection create an illusion of objective scholarly authority, complete with cross-references via the book's recurring characters; *The Quantity Theory of Insanity* needs only an index to complete the facade. Self provides footnotes, a numerical reference marker for a nonexisting endnote, and a selected bibliography of scholarly articles pertaining to the theory at the end of the Ford's putative document. Such features demonstrate Self's own narrative mischief, identifying him as an impish and intrusive presence prone to "constructing elaborate *trompe l'oeil* effects" (102) akin to those of Alkan's naughty protégées and other metafictional writers. The bibliography itself functions as a microcosm of this satire, revealing that for all his claims to authority Harold Ford published his monograph on the Quantity Theory through a vanity press while the other entries mock the titles and subjects of scholarly research projects. It also reiterates a common assumption regarding the discursive and practical failures of contemporary critical theory, a field upon which Self draws at times in his narrative style.

The titles of many of the papers mentioned in the story have the dual quality of appearing crushingly banal and strikingly authentic. Even the purportedly influential *British Journal of Ephemera* (*BJE*), which like Busner and other characters pops up time and again in Self's fiction, encodes in its title the utter insignificance of the research activities that these practitioners spend their careers inflating from projects of intellectual marginalia to grand social theories. Presented as facile and self-absorbed, academia and its attendant theories and research areas appear in Self's fiction as a particular form of indulgent decadence. As Self presents the academic milieu, it is not one simply of frumpy dons cloistered away in isolating, vine-covered Gothic buildings but one of beige-and-gray institutions and suburban detached houses—in the center of society and yet, paradoxically, even more remote from it than the stereotypical metaphor of the ivory tower would seem to suggest. As Steven Connor demonstrates, the university has complicated relationships with outside society, existing as "both an asocial enclave, protected from the uncertainties and excesses of the social, and yet also a scale model of it, a burnished surface on which the dangerous and pre-dictable lines of force of the social and political world may be seen faintly but finely incised."[13] Self expands this relationship to encompass not only British society but humanity as understood by an academic. In "Understanding the Ur-Bororo," Self satirizes the academic world through anthropology rather than clinical psychology.

In "Understanding the Ur-Bororo," Reigate, a redbrick univer-sity located on the periphery of Surrey's North Downs, provides the educational backdrop for Self's pastiche of a conventional bildungsroman. By creating a burlesque of this genre, he deftly critiques the conventions of the coming-of-age story while ap-pearing to meet readers' expectations for a first book of fiction. Self presents an anonymous first-person narrator who in the story's expository paragraphs recounts his student days and his bonding with a fellow loner named Janner. Not quite best friends, the two were thrown together in a pairing of defiance, "Janner and I versus the entire faculty and entire student body combined" (69). With the privilege of a decade of experience, the narrator finds the ability to place this friendship and its effect on him in perspective: "although it was my maturity that was at issue," he says, "it is Janner who is the central character of this story" (70). Unlike Dickens's David Copperfield, who asserts that his autobiography itself will determine whether or not he can be the hero of his own story, this narrator is eclipsed by the man who helps prompt the narrator's belated rite of passage.

Bright and ambitious, Janner is first depicted as someone who could have flourished in the proper intellectual environment, implying that Reigate did little to foster such qualities. Yet Jan-ner succeeds, ultimately becoming "The Anthropologist" just as

Harold Ford imagines himself as an *"ubermensch"* and prime
Quantity Theoretician (99). The connection between Janner
and Ford seems deliberate, and in "The Quantity Theory of
Insanity" Self reveals that they know each other. Whereas the
narrator's sympathetic image of his friend excuses one of Janner's most "repulsive" idiosyncrasies, "the way catarrh gurgled
and huffed up and down his windpipe when he was speaking"
(70), Ford is far less forgiving of this slobbering eccentricity as
he spies Janner in attendance at the conference that closes
"Quantity Theory": "Janner is a repellant individual, with
something of Alkan about him—the way he tilts his head back
in order to slurp the catarrh down his throat is especially striking" (148). The fact that Janner appears in both stories is
significant not simply for the continuity of his ingestive man-
nerism but because his presence compels Ford to acknowledge
uncertainty. "I have no idea why he has chosen to be in Denver," Ford remarks (148). This aside is a revealing comment
and a key to Self's narrative technique: his characters are victims of Self's maneuverings, giving them glimpses of the fact
that their own free will is illusory as they are manipulated by
the author's own designs. But Janner, unlike Busner and the
other therapists involved with the Quantity Theory, remains
indifferent to its appeal: even in his student days he "was
unmoved by the relativistic, structuralist and post-structuralist
theories of anthropology with their painful concern with the
effect of the observer on the observed" (72).

Early in "Understanding the Ur-Bororo" the narrator
alludes to Shakespeare, drawing attention to the work's dramatic qualities. Comparing Janner to Prospero from *The Tem-
pest* (69), he sees his friend as a wizard amid the stilted groves
of academe. Set against the narrator's studies in geography and

physical education (70), Janner's philosophical interests in anthropology make him an attractive and compelling intellectual figure, so attractive that the narrator confesses to being "a little bit in love with him" (74). Yet if Janner reminds the narrator of Prospero, particularly through his pursuit of knowledge, he must have a counterpart, his Caliban. Self twists the allusion by shunning an image of the wild, brutish side of human nature, presenting instead a remote tribe of Amazonian bores.

Janner travels to South America only to encounter a group of individuals strikingly similar to the British. The Ur-Bororo, whose name alludes to the Bororo tribe that Claude Levi-Strauss discusses in *Tristes Tropiques* (1955), but more importantly phonically evokes an impression of malaise, inhabit a culture of stasis. This is characteristically marked by endless feelings of apathy and ennui. Through their idle deeds and words the Ur-Bororo readily acknowledge these traits and further reveal them in the tribe's perception of its own makeup. Janner explains to the narrator the etymological significance of the tribe's name: "'Ur-Bororo' is a convenient translation of the name neighbouring tribes use for them, which simply means 'here before the Bororo.' The Ur-Bororo actually refer to themselves as 'The People Who You Wouldn't Like to Be Cornered by at a Party.' They view other tribal peoples as leading infinitely more alluring lives than themselves, and often speak, not without a trace of hurt feelings, of the many parties and other social events to which they are never invited" (82). Ironically Janner, who at Reigate was already on track to maturing into a "pure observer" and "ultimate voyeur" (72), did not need to visit the South American rainforest for his field research; his work in the "suburban jungle" (80) of southern England, where he examined the social habits of commuters, tradespeople, and other average citizens, including a study of the psychogeography of launderettes (77), achieved similar findings.

The Ur-Bororo, it transpires, had first been discovered by Dr. Lurie, whose Lurie Foundation endows the Anthropology Department at Reigate and funds the research of Janner, and before him his research adviser, Dr. Marston. Lurie, Marston, and Janner form the entire body of field researchers devoted to understanding the Ur-Bororo. All papers in the Lurie Archive at the British Library are held in a closed stack, available only to the limited number of researchers involved in studying the tribe. This stipulation, Janner eventually divulges, stems from Lurie's desire that others share the same experience he had with these insipid natives, a desire that dismisses the necessity for researchers to publish their work—including a required paper of a minimum of 30,000 words—on the Ur-Bororo: "All Lurie wanted was for some other poor idiot to suffer the unbelievable tedium he experienced when staying with the Ur-Bororo in the Thirties" (91). However, despite the supposition of the Ur-Bororo—and the British—as a unique society, this same monotony forms the underlying premise of the story and gives the narrator his epiphanic rite of passage.

Describing his adult life after Reigate, the narrator couches it in terms of moderation, passivity, and dullness (74–75). The similarity of his life to that of the Ur-Bororo is made more apparent by the presence of Janner's Ur-Bororo wife, Jane, and her brother, David. That they experienced no problems assimilating to English culture further buttresses the story's premise, revealing the stark similarities in both societies. Instead of condoning a kind of generic, stereotypical Waspishness, through his satirical method Self condemns what the novelist Angus Wilson branded as Anglo-Saxon attitudes.

Physically, linguistically, socially, and religiously, the Ur-Bororo and the British appear indistinguishable. It is notable that Self christens these characters Jane and David: both names reappear in his fiction as emblematic of English mediocrity. Liorah Anne Golomb draws a similar conclusion in her explication of Self's major works, observing that "'Dave' indicates the unspectacular, the undistinguished; conformity, niceness, perhaps; in a word, stereotyped middle-class English life."[14] Likewise, "Jane" conveys much the same impression, one that becomes doubled with the marriage of Jane and Janner. Because Self renders the banality of modern Englishness through a consistent nomenclature, the anonymity of the narrator in "Understanding the Ur-Bororo" suggests that this figure has become wholly indistinguishable, undergoing an elision of personal identity. This transformation inverts the typical pattern of a bildungsroman by charting how the narrator has throughout his adulthood shed all markings of individuality, effectively eradicating his ego.

CHAPTER THREE

Hermaphrodites and Hermeneutics
Cock & Bull

In 1992 Will Self followed *The Quantity Theory of Insanity* with a pair of novellas published jointly as *Cock & Bull*. With the relative lack of sales potential for shorter fiction compared to that of the novel, this was something of a risky move for Self and his publishers, but the form suits him well. In terms of rhythm and pacing especially, Self's expressive style finds accordance with this slippery form. Novellas in general defy easy definition, accommodating works that range from approximately fifty to well over a hundred pages in length. The difference between these two modes rests not simply with length but with degree of character development and often a reliance upon an episodic versus more extended narrative structure.

Cock & Bull is a grotesque comedy that destabilizes conventional realist modes of narrative representation as it presents a sardonic examination of gender distinctions. Generally the "grotesque" in literature refers to exaggerated deviations from the accepted ideas of natural order and proportion, becoming instead absurd, bizarre, and freakish; it appears frequently in the works of François Rabelais, Jonathan Swift, Nikolai Gogol, Franz Kafka, and others in satirical representations of the body. While Self follows these writers in this loose tradition, perhaps the most notable antecedent is Philip Roth, whose 1972 novella *The Breast* describes the transmogrification of his protagonist, David Kepesh, into an enormous mammary gland.

Self also applies aspects of the grotesque to his mode of narration, using in "Cock" a first-person narrator that gives way at times to the voice and intimidating presence of the novella's protagonist, who in turn violates both the narrator's and the reader's suspension of disbelief. This doubling of competing voices results in a kind of gender-neutral narrative.

Both "Cock" and "Bull" constitute acerbic satires on gender identity, works in which abrupt changes to sexual physiology force their principal characters to confront the arbitrary nature of gender identity. While this is certainly a dominant theme linking these two novellas it is not the sole object of Self's satire. To different extents each of the novellas deals with the nature of writing and the relevance of fiction to life. Self has called *Cock & Bull* "an elaborate joke about the failure of narrative,"[1] a conceit that is most prominent in the opening story, "Cock: A Novelette." Although comparisons to the absurdist irony underlying Kafka's "The Metamorphosis" are apt and seemingly inevitable, Self delves even further into literary history for his precursors in these works. With these novellas Self presents himself as a late-twentieth-century Ovid, using metaphors of abrupt metamorphoses to explain human transformations, a motif that reappears in later works as well. Themes of interpretation permeate *Cock & Bull*, emphasizing the manners in which the body, personal and social identities, and narrative texts are construed and frequently misread by others.

"Cock" describes the transformation of Carol, a passive, dull young woman in her university years, into a frustrated wife and then into an aged, violent man resembling a "sardonic, effete don,"[2] an evolution that initially requires just over three years to complete. That is, Carol and Dan, her husband, are together for exactly three years, and her penis attains its full maturity when she is twenty-one; it is unclear how much time elapses between the events Carol describes and the moment she recounts them on a train coach, and while it is possible that a span of approximately twenty years has elapsed (15) between the events and their narration, Carol's ultimate physical resemblance to a man in late middle-age seems most likely an example of descriptive hyperbole. The principal source of her aggression is presented as the penis she sprouts unexpectedly, a weapon she uses along with linguistic tools to assault and humiliate her victims. Conversely, "Bull" depicts the saga of a hearty magazine section editor named John Bull who equally unexpectedly has a fully formed vagina appear in the pit behind one of his knees. These physical and psychological transformations portray the latent instability of social roles and identities, including one's sense of selfhood. As with Ovid and Kafka, Self gives expression in the form of physical change to the emotional and psychological fluctuations people experience, showing how easily barriers that were presumed to be firm might be traversed. The subject matter and Self's caustic satirical aims in *Cock & Bull* virtually ensure divergent responses.

Upon publication the book received mixed reviews, and Self became the focus of the sort of hostile critical attention that also attended the publication of his following books. Writing for the *TLS*, Natasha Walter called the book "a minor disaster," insisting that "it is in the language, the nuts and bolts of his prose, that Self has most clearly lost control."[3] Walter's review concedes brilliance to *The Quantity Theory of Insanity*, but, she implies, this appears to have been a fluke, and she takes issue with Self's critical standing. In his *London Review of Books* assessment of *Cock & Bull*, Anthony Quinn strikes a more moderate tone than Walter's hasty dismissal, praising Self's narrative abilities and "virtuoso expressiveness" in the book: "No question, there is some wonderfully fluent riffing throughout *Cock & Bull;* open at almost any page and you can find a language that is vividly textured and ingeniously cross-referenced. . . . Yet for all its singularity, the experience of *Cock & Bull* fades very quickly: not so much a meditation on gender politics as a bizarre and calculatedly repellent party-turn."[4] But it is on precisely the book's depictions of gender politics that gender theorists have focused.

Janet Harbord, for instance, sees in *Cock & Bull* and Jeanette Winterson's novel *Written on the Body* a correlation between the ways in which these works of fiction examine gender and the effects they produce as a result: "First [contemporary writing on gender] suggests in a potentially subversive way the constructed nature of gender. Second, it stages the causal debate of the gender-body-sexuality triad. Is it the body that mutates, invoking a shift in gender, and finally impacting on society? Or is it gender identification that shifts, invoking a change in corporeality, thus opening out the possibilities of sexual practice?"[5] Moreover, she proclaims, *Cock & Bull* "can be read as a staging of these debates without imposing closure." Crucially, however, the novellas are not concerned solely with gender identification. The real concerns the book presents lie in its blend of narrative quandaries and issues surrounding gender construction, in addition to the problems concerning interpretation that these facets present.

Essentially a pair of updated, ribald shaggy-dog stories in the vein of the grand eighteenth-century satirists Laurence Sterne and Jonathan Swift, the novellas' function in this genre becomes apparent, as Self explicitly—and ironically—declares. "This is what you get if you sit there like a prat," a policeman tells the narrator of "Cock" at the end of the novella, "listening to a load of cock . . . and bull" (145). As with the French *coq-à-l'âne,* cock-and-bull or shaggy-dog stories are absurd in nature, frequently canards that play on the patience of their audience. In such seemingly pointless yarns the reader or listener becomes the subject of the author's mischievous narrative joke. By making his reader the object, if not victim, of this extended joke, Self effectively demonstrates an enduring—and potentially abusive—authority that the author and narrator wield over the reader. Exploiting the concept of authorial omnipotence, Self has Carol disingenuously insist that "there is no hidden hand in this tail [*sic*]; there is no lurking, shadowy narrator. What I tell you—that is the truth. *Allah Akbar,* you understand? I am a man of God. I speak the truth—God's truth. 'There is no God but God'" (83). Harbord detects an underlying subversive purpose to Self's displacement of authority in identifying "Bull," for example, as a farce in its subtitle. She draws a connection between Self's metaphorical depictions of genitalia and the rape episodes in each of the novellas, finding a "distancing irony" in his depiction of gender and sex roles, thus "foregrounding his own relative power precisely for us to resist, mock, laugh at . . . thereby displacing this authority."[6] This narrative distancing is important, especially given Self's own admission to have written the novella "out of rage at the involuntary character of my own sexual arousal."[7] His authority, however, is displaced only superficially, dictating the powerlessness that his narrator experiences.

"Cock" contains a double-tier perspective in which the supposed third-person narrative that forms the majority of the novella appears in roman type and the first-person narrative by an unnamed male speaker appears in italics. In actuality the novella consists of twin first-person accounts; in the roman-type passages the narrator alleges details that would require some degree of intimate knowledge—whether as an omniscient narrator or first-person speaker— regarding Carol's personal history, and it transpires that this donnish effeminate speaker is the resexualized Carol. She/he appears dissociated from his/her previous identity as Carol, justifying the use of a third-person masculine point of view and its covertly biased perspective. Readers should not disregard the egotism Carol displays in presenting his/her life in the third person, in this case a sham perspective that signals the narrator's awkward attempt to create an impression of rhetorical gravity. The shifts between speakers are signaled by space breaks in the paragraph structure, becoming increasingly frequent as the masculine Carol is whipped into a frenzy of sexual and verbal violence at the prospect of committing an imminent rape. The duration of the interruptions becomes increasingly staccato, ultimately representing the malicious speaker's orgasm as the two formerly distinct points of view alternate within single paragraphs (142–43). This exchange between the doubled narrators—or narrator and putative narratee—mimics and subverts the traditional author-reader relationship. Further complicating this web, Carol expresses her desire to inhabit a central realm between binary narrative positions, to be protagonist and antagonist alike (101) of this "repellant tale" (14). Rather than the loss of narrative control that Natasha Walter detects in the novellas, these brutal passages exemplify Self's attempts to subvert his readers' conceptions of traditional narrative techniques while simultaneously striving to erode equally preconceived ideas of gender and authority.

By the time Self began writing *Cock & Bull,* for him the abstract notion of masculinity had long been wrought up with belligerence, an unfortunate inheritance his mother bequeathed him during his adolescence. "Whether because of my mother's espoused feminism, or her obvious misanthropy, I was helped early on to the conclusion that almost all there was to masculinity was the delineation of one's sexuality in terms of aggression," he remarks in *Perfidious Man*, a book that places Self's revealing essay alongside a series of photographs by David Gamble that capture the wide varieties of masculine identity and an additional text by Stephen Whittle, a female-to-male transsexual and campaigner for transsexual rights. "Fucking and fighting, or fucking as fighting, or fighting as fucking. My own father was, according to my mother, so much less than a man; a conscientious objector in the war, who couldn't have put up a set of shelves if his life depended on it. In their relationship he supplied the fucking—she the fighting. They were a schizophrenic hermaphrodite; their marriage a screaming Procrustes, always stretched to breaking point—and beyond."[8] Given the intense emotional reverberations that Self's familial background has produced and which resonate throughout his work, it is plausible to view *Cock & Bull* as a semicathartic volume, but it is foremost playfully satiric rather than personal or political.

Despite its vivid harshness "Cock" remains in essence a grotesque comic fable. Part of its subversive nature, in fact, lies in Self's reworking of traditional literary genres and themes, including the bildungsroman as well as the cock-and-bull story. In "Cock," Carol—whose name suggests Lewis Carroll, a seminal influence on Self's interest in transmogrification—develops from a submissive, sexually frustrated young woman into a masculine sexual predator. At college in Wales, she studied sociology, completing one third of her degree requirements, and before meeting the man whom she would marry, "Carol had spent long, Sapphic nights under the influence of a rotund lesbian called Beverley" (4). During her sexual encounters with Beverley and male lovers, Carol failed to reach an orgasm, a feat that Dan, her future husband, achieves "by a fluke" one evening after a pub crawl with Dan's mates (4). The experience is significant: "It was that brief, ecstatic lancing and its subsequent balmy wave that had wedded Carol to Dan, and despite the fact that the experience had not been repeated Carol still felt obscurely bonded to him" (7). At nineteen, a year after this blissful incident, Carol married Dan, two years her senior. Her naïveté in marrying him because of this single experience reveals itself after they move to London and Carol realizes that not only was the orgasm a fluke—one that is denoted as a fortuitous achievement on Dan's part, showing Carol's passive nature and perceptions of sexuality that assign success and failure alike to a single partner—but that "she felt less of a woman when Dan was around" (9), an ironic epiphany that also serves as the novella's opening line.

In London, Carol and Dan establish a caricature of a supposedly traditional domestic arrangement where the wife tends to the house, intellectually bored and sexually thwarted, while the husband earns their living. By presenting this from Carol's perspective, Self is able to quickly present such socially prescribed gender roles as incongruous with individuality. When not working, Dan, whom Carol comes to view as "slight, sour, effete, unsure of himself" (9), spends his time with his friends in lengthy boozing sessions. The drinking takes a toll on his and Carol's "cramped and pedestrian sex-life" (11). After his drunkenness reaches its lowest point, Dan swears off drinking and the raucous companionship of his "mates" Gary, Barry, Derry, Gerry, and Dave 1, replacing them with sobriety under the guidance of a man named Dave Hobbes, nicknamed Dave 2.

Dave 2's given name reflects Self's background in philosophy, suggestively combining the names of David Hume and Thomas

Hobbes. More crucially, given the significance of the name "Dave" in Self's fiction as an indicator of uncompromising banality, the fact that Dan replaces one Dave with another amplifies the triteness of his life. A "parasite of the emotions" (66), Dave 2 finds a peculiar satisfaction in simulating empathy with Carol and Dan. His "psycho-empathetic voyeurism" (67) serves as a substitute for sexual gratification and emotional stimulation, and Carol begins to feel uneasy in his presence. Dave 2's parasitic voyeurism—which leads ultimately and disastrously to a more direct experience with the newly virile Carol—is more than the characteristic tic of a creepy character but a metaphor representing the readers' participation as spectators, just as the hazy line between speaker and author frequently dissolves into further ambiguity.

"That's your style, isn't it," the transformed Carol berates his/her audience of one in an isolated and—inexplicably—prewar train compartment. "Being clever and allusive, but what does this really amount to save for trying to get one over on good, ordinary, straightforward people?" (71). Self presents with heavy irony what can be read fairly as critiques of his fictional methods. He jokingly posits the presumption of his readers as innocent victims, "good, ordinary, straightforward people" at whose expense he perpetrates an act of narrative mischief by violating implied boundaries between author and reader. Such transgressions include the elimination of descriptive realism for a narrative that travesties such approaches, the abolition of psychological verisimilitude in favor of a metafictional frame of self-reference, and the loss of stability that a reliable narrator allows. Not that Self's references are all inward: like much of his fiction, "Cock" is a highly allusive novella, freighted with direct and indirect cultural and literary references. This mixture of so-called high- and low-cultural references, expressed in a style that synthesizes these two poles in its blend of Mandarin and popular vernacular formulations, is at the core of Self's style. Such pairings are not unique and can be found in much of modernist and postmodern literature. In one respect Self is carrying forward the tradition that T. S. Eliot, Ezra Pound, James Joyce, and other early-twentieth-century writers helped to inaugurate. These are qualities that Carol claims to abhor: "I faintly despise the oblique and distorting innovations of the modern . . . don't you? I like something to be straightforward. I like a story to tell me no more or no less than the storyteller intends. I don't go looking for hidden meanings, I don't try and pick away at the surface of things, pretending to find some 'psychological' sub-structure that really I have placed there myself, by dint of sleight-of-mind" (102).

Despite the multiple levels of narrative manipulation, "Cock" retains an iota of pathos. Its story is not simply one of genital augmentation; it charts the gradual loss of Carol's essential self. As her strange "frond" matures into a fullscale penis it entails the elision of Carol's previous identity, a further transformation for which, unsurprisingly, she is ill prepared. She becomes a sadistic and destructive being, leaving behind her a trail of shattered egos, lives, and readers' assumptions about storytelling. Carol's excitement at wielding her penis as a weapon dissolves into frenetic violence as she molests and in the process murders Dan. Furthermore, once her transformation is complete, Carol becomes a virulent racist and anti-Semite. Underlying her ultimate viciousness in the humiliation that accompanies her violent assaults is a sense of rage that has shed its inhibitions, an anger that is not necessarily confined to the story's fictional characters. Through Carol, Self appears to be giving voice and actions to a personal set of frustrations, most especially those concerning both gender and fiction. Noting his responses to people who would inquire about what "Cock" is "about," Self writes in *Perfidious Man* that

> I'd give two answers: that it was about my rage with feminist arguments that all men were rapists by virtue of possessing the requisite weapon; that it was about the breakdown in gender distinctions which implied that all it was to be either one or the other was a mix and match of the requisite parts; that it was about my own nature, for, as Cocteau remarked, all true artists are hermaphrodites.
>
> But I knew then—and know still better now—that it was about none and all of these things; that it was about my own vexed relationship with my gender; that it was about this strange situation we find ourselves in at the moment in Western societies. . . . And it's often seemed to me that we are in the interregnum between two systems of sexuality, and that the strangest phenomena are arising.[9]

Carol's hermaphroditism embodies multiple dualities, the double-pronged existences of sex, gender, and even fiction itself, all thrown into an uneasy amalgamation. During the course of her transformation Self illustrates the conflicts that can arise when these dualities rub against one another or collide unexpectedly.

In *Cock & Bull*, Self provides clear clues to his narrative intentions through his choice of epigraphs just as he does through each work's subtitles. He sets the theme of "Cock" by selecting a passage from Canto 10 of Byron's *Don Juan*, a choice that reflects Self's satirical and descriptive aims in the novella. Byron's speaker eschews description and refuses to "philosophize," effectively disengaging himself from narrative expectations much in the way

Self's narrators do, and Byron's image of thought clinging persistently to the speaker "through the abyss / Of this odd labyrinth" provides an advance clue regarding Self's narrative tangle. The epigraph to "Bull," however, depends on the reader construing a Freudian interpretation from the opening lines of Tennyson's *Maud*, a passage that describes the suicide of the speaker's father but also evokes images of female sexual maturity by suggesting simultaneously menstruation and defloration. Tennyson's images of "the dreadful hollow behind the little wood," its "lips . . . dabbled with blood-red heath,"[10] and the fact that the cliff's "red ribb'd ledges drip with a silent horror of blood" (1–3) assume additional ironic sexual connotations in light of Bull's eventual "vitrified hymen" (258) and his firsthand experience of female biology, what Carol in "Cock" regards as "the bloody horror of gynaecological fact" (31). Vaginal jokes and images are central to "Bull," a novella that stands in a converse and complementary relationship to its predecessor.

"Bull: A Farce" centers on John Bull, a "thirty-something" man (178) whose name evokes stereotypical images of English patriotism and self-image. His name refers to the personified image of British nationalism that John Arbuthnot, a member of the Scriblerus Club along with Swift, Alexander Pope, and John Gay, used in his satiric political pamphleteering. Self's John Bull is in many respects a more realistic portrait of the modern male psyche than the frequently simplistic images that appear in much of popular culture and fiction. Rather than an aggressive yob, or thug, a personification of atavistic male vigor, or a timid "wet," Self creates a character who exhibits aspects of each of these types. Bull is large and athletic, with a passion for sports in general and rugby in particular. For much of the novella Bull works as the cabaret editor for a listings magazine called *Get Out!*, a barely veiled version of *Time Out!,* and his ignorance of the theater and performance art causes his reviews to be laden with clichéd sports analogies. One assignment, to review the act of a misogynistic stand-up comic called Razza Rob who introduces his crude vaginal jokes with his catchphrase "Doncha wanna know," might have elicited his sexual transmogrification.

As Bull leaves abruptly during Razza Rob's performance the jockstrap-clad comic selects him for ridicule: "Whaddya call a man with a cunt in the back of his leg? . . . Fucked if I know, but any port in a storm, eh old chep?" (170–71). Self never directly states in "Bull" that this explains Bull's sexual peculiarity. Although Self intimates as much, through his narrator he states explicitly that the more important consideration is that it happened to Bull, an ideal candidate for this extraordinary mutation:

> Who can say whether Razza Rob, like some obscene magus, had inflicted the vagina on Bull. A magical curse pointing up the involuted redundancy of their common sexuality. Who can say? It does seem fitting however, apt. There would be no point in implanting a vagina in the back of just any man's knee. You might get some scion of raised consciousness; some almost-Iron John; some acquaintance of Dorothy longing to become a friend. No. Much better that this be just a *congruence* understood by us. And much better that it should be Bull, the dubious Bull, the shy Bull, the *conditioned* Bull, who had to bear the weight of this unacceptable transmogrification. (171–72)

Put simply, Bull's ingrained psychological resistance to being identified as feminine marks him out as a model case for this experiment in fictional genetic and social engineering. This passage is atypical of "Bull" in that Self's narrator steps forward to directly address the integrity of the story and to subvert realistic considerations such as omniscience, expository development, and causality.

In comparison to "Cock," "Bull" seems to be much more of a conventional story, containing a linear plot and avoiding the complications of stratified points of view. Self only occasionally breaks the veil of his implied authorial third-person perspective to address the reader directly through rhetorical questions concerning the story's plausibility, or to offer an alternative fantasy scene rather than the purported truth of the events. Whereas in "Cock" metafictional commentary and motifs remain vital to the fabric of story and plot, in "Bull" such moments seem more awkwardly contrived without benefit of any substantial self-reflective irony. With its pithy epilogue, "Bull" seems in many respects to mirror the "straightforward" type of story replete with coda that the donlike Carol avers to favor in "Cock" (102). Together these two novellas present a paradox concerning mimetic premises by suggesting in one that traditional realism is nearing obsolescence and in the other that a realistic veneer can bolster the fantastic aspect of the work's primary conceit. As often as Self challenges the reader's ability or will to suspend disbelief, rather than exhaustively undermining the practice he implies that suspending disbelief remains a key component of the storytelling process. Accordingly Self frequently tilts the onus by demanding that the reader imagine this fictional universe in spite of the fabulous and fabricated basis he systematically lays bare. These apparently divergent narrative paths have been at the root of theoretical debates on fictional methods for decades, most intensely since the advent of postmodernism and Alain Robbe-Grillet's conception of the *noveau roman*, or "new novel." Self's fiction proposes a reconciliation of these contradictory methods as a fundamentally hermaphroditic entity.[11]

One other crucial distinction between "Cock" and "Bull" involves the incongruous sexual organs that each of the respective protagonists acquires. Carol's growth of a penis is certainly a striking phenomenon, as is Bull's vaginal development, but it remains essentially a destructive appendage. Bull, conversely, gains a complete and fully functional set of female reproductive organs, compacted to fit into his left leg. As a result he experiences hormonal fluctuations, increased feelings of vulnerability, menstruation, and pregnancy and childbirth. His altered sexual biology thus becomes generative rather than destructive, and through the process he sustains his basic psychological temperament. Bull's sexual hybridity forces him to contend with and to accept his genital abnormality as he attempts to conceal it and its corresponding gender characteristics from public scrutiny.

Self also depicts psychological hermaphroditism in the form of bisexuality. In "Bull" sexual identity stems predominantly from the characters' own ideas of how they see themselves and how they wish others to see them. Bull's sexual experience is somewhat limited and intercourse contains for him a neurotic component. Wary of emotional attachments, Bull possesses a "fundamental diffidence" regarding sex, a reticence that prompts him to select as partners "individuals whose sexuality was already fatally compromised and detached from the gender specific" (209), a type characterized in the novella by a freelance contributor to Bull's magazine (and his eventual replacement) named Juniper. In the absence of proximity to such equally neurotic partners, Bull's sexual practice is restricted to masturbation. This changes when he is seduced by his doctor, Alan Margoulies.

As a general practitioner in north London, Margoulies has assiduously constructed a perception of himself as a conscientious doctor, one whose tireless dedication to his patients —which includes routine house calls for services that other caregivers could easily provide—has impelled various staff members and patients to view him as a candidate for sainthood. Margoulies cultivates this public persona to buttress his practice and to conceal aspects of his personal life. Outwardly Margoulies's life appears admirable; his practice at the Grove Health Centre is flourishing, and he seems to have an ideal family life. Yet while he might appear to his wife, Naomi, to be conscientious, he is also described as "not nice at all—egotistic, domineering, aggressive and duplicitous" (160). It is largely a combination of these qualities that compels Margoulies to abjure his professional ethics, becoming "a silent signatory of the hypocritic oath" (188), in order to seduce Bull.

Margoulies initially conceals from his patient the actuality of Bull's vagina. Although he knows that ethically he should refer Bull to a specialist, Margoulies instead informs Bull that the supposed injury is a combination of a wound and burn. To prolong this deception he prescribes Valium to Bull, which would further enable the seduction. Margoulies is "addicted to the pornographic whimsy of his own silly imagination" (163), a fantasy life that includes scenarios involving his penetration of vaginas that had yet to suffer the physical trauma of childbirth. He does not initially feel lust at the sight of Bull's genital abnormality, and in a vain attempt to erase from his mind a litany of thoughts revolving around Bull's vagina he consults reference works where he might find proof of previous cases similar to Bull. The trust that Bull displays toward Margoulies spurs thoughts of protection—or so the reputedly conscientious doctor attempts to convince himself—and Margoulies begins to view Bull as distinctly feminine. In fact he starts to imagine the topography of the London motorways as conforming to a crude female design, a vast body that he can speedily penetrate in his car with its phallic aerials (241–42). As he enters Bull's flat in East Finchley, Margoulies begins to wrestle with his self-image and sexual attraction for Bull (221). To accept that he might entertain homosexual fantasies would undermine all that Margoulies believed about himself and wanted others to believe about him as well. He eventually comes to acknowledge "his lust for what it was: a closet queen, parading in the assumed pasteboard refinery of love" (298).

Likewise for Bull, his seduction greatly alters his own self-image. The experience is "shattering" for him: "Bull felt violated, traduced, seduced, bamboozled, subjugated, entrapped and enfolded. He felt his capacity for action surgically removed. He felt, for the first time in his life, that his sense of himself as a purposeful automaton, striding on the world's stage, had been completely vitiated by a warm wash of transcendence" (234). Self's sardonic, dark humor risks at times being perceived as simply tasteless, a prime example of which is found in Bull's perceptions of his defloration. Bull likens the shards of his "vitrified hymen" to a broken window that he passes during a walk through London, and through an example of indirect discourse his seduction by the Jewish Margoulies is referred to as a "bizarre inversion of *Kristallnacht*" (258). In his review of *My Idea of Fun*, Craig Seligman looks back to this passage as representative of the problems with Self's comic impulses. Noting that Self's mother was Jewish, Seligman argues that this fact "makes his little stab at a Holocaust joke less stupefying. But it doesn't make it any funnier."[12]

Throughout of the remaining portions of "Bull," Margoulies and Bull enter into a relationship that parodies adulterous trysts. Their affair remains clandestine, conducted under a public subterfuge of male friendship. In the process Self intimates that to view one set of male-male relationships as socially prescribed and another set as socially proscribed is itself absurd. In the story's epilogue Bull is seen initially as a social fugitive, fleeing London for San Francisco where, with the aid of "exorbitant hush money" paid by his rugby insurance policy (309) he is able to give birth to the son Margoulies sired. Self presents this flight to a California clinic in the story's seemingly conventional uplifting coda, rescuing Bull from the annihilation that appeared to await him following his realization that Margoulies would remain with his wife. Rather than committing suicide, as Bull intended, he reconstructs his life in such a way to conform to social expectations. Bull opens a sporting goods and memorabilia shop in Cardiff, where despite not being Welsh he is accepted and his son, Kenneth, becomes "popular with the local kids, very much one of the boys" (310).

Is social acceptance simply the result of not challenging a community's principles? *Cock & Bull* affirms as much. "Bull" in particular presents various communities—medical, athletic, urban, gender—where to be socially included one must disguise any individual characteristic that might be regarded as peculiar or abnormal. Homogeneity is thus an illusion that is built and maintained by communal acquiescence.

Cock & Bull provided a glimpse of what a full-length Will Self novel might look like. Beyond the mutual north London settings there is a sophisticated cohesion and continuity in these novellas. Carol, "an ersatz ancient mariner" (14), is all too willing to confess her past and deeds, and even attends Dan's

Alcoholics Anonymous meetings where participants routinely bare their shame; Bull, on the other hand, feels alienated, "unable to confess his true nature," and longs to join a "Vaginas Anonymous" support group (262). Where Carol longs for children after leaving Wales for London (11), Bull becomes an initially reluctant mother and leaves London to eventually reside in Wales. Specific phrases repeat throughout *Cock & Bull* in notable variations, subtly forging the novellas into a unified work. Thus beneath Carol's accent, which foreshadows Bull's public-school inflections, is a "chassis" that "had perhaps been spot-welded by elocution lessons" (15); Ramona tells Bull of his/her past as a spotwelder at a shipyard (274); and when Bull recalls his sexual tryst with Juniper he thinks of how her "hard chassis of crotch 'n' bum 'n' thighs had hammered down on to him" (207). For Carol a *petit mort* is an orgasm metaphor, but for Bull the term signifies a loss of self (229).

Most significantly "Frond" denotes both Carol's nascent penis (32, 33) and the plaster in Alan Margoulies's office (180); the term functions as an objective correlative for the emotional trauma Carol and Bull face with their genital anomalies. In his review, Tom Shone notes that such "universal joint adjectives and all-purpose nouns, which flip so easily between human and inhuman, micro- and macrocosm, are the real cross-dressers in *Cock & Bull*."[13] Similar repetitions occur within each work and between the two novellas. However, in one careless breach of continuity Self has Bull driving an "ancient Mini Cooper" (173), which later undergoes its own mysterious transformation into a Volkswagen Beetle (249). The pattern of repetitions works as a frame of reference with each occurrence functioning as a virtual road marker, a point Self has observed in J. G. Ballard's narrative methods: "a writer's body of work, taken as a whole, is a kind of aerial shot of a foreign territory through which you are conducting the reader . . . a sense in which all these topographies join up in some other, numinous parallel world. . . . And the repetitions are, therefore, the switches directing the reader back into this other world."[14]

If Self has attempted to raise questions concerning predominant ideas about sex, gender, and the function of fictional narrative, he also raises questions about his own methods as a writer —questions that resurface with his follow-up to *Cock & Bull.* As the publication date for Self's first novel, *My Idea of Fun,* drew near, he took stock of his own work and aesthetic objectives. His first three books were essentially masculine in character and point of view; his next stage, he decided, should address family life, beyond his roles as husband and father. The sanguine depiction of family life at the close of "Bull" perhaps signals this transition. "I don't want to be a Boy's Own writer," Self has said. "Too many people read my books and assume I'm a solo male. It's understandable because so far I've been picking over my early 20s in my fiction, but family life is an advantage: now I hope to move on and write books which reflect that. No more male narrators. I'm not going to write another until I get a feminine perspective right."[15]

CHAPTER FOUR

Empathy for the Devil

My Idea of Fun

The career of the Roman poet Virgil, progressing linearly through shorter lyric forms and the pastoral before tackling the demands of the epic form in his *Aeneid,* seemed to later poets such as Dante, Edmund Spenser, and John Milton a sound method of becoming a major poet. Will Self seems to have followed a similar progression, advancing successively through the formal hierarchies of the short story and novella before publishing a novel. As with many first novels, Self's *My Idea of Fun* (1994) falls into the narrative genre of the bildungsroman, the German term for a novel of education or development. These works, which frequently include a strong element of autobiography, portray the process of the central character experiencing various successes and failures, personally and socially, as he or she attains maturity and establishes a firm identity. Self has made profitable use of his past in short stories such as "The North London Book of the Dead," but he avoids transparent autobiography. His tendency in his shorter fiction has been to portray experience as speculative rather than directly lived, which makes the introspective qualities in *My Idea of Fun* all the more surprising.

Although Self's first novel is often understood as a satire on an age of capitalist excess, its personal revelations confront matters of deep concern for Self that continue to crop up in one fashion or another in his subsequent fiction. Instead of standing aloof from his subject matter and characters, Self closes the psychological distance between author and protagonist. Subtitled "A Cautionary Tale," *My Idea of Fun* contains a moral allegory concerning the psychopathology of addiction—a postmodern parable that transcends the novel's satirical aspects.

Self has said that the kernel of *My Idea of Fun* "is the similarity I see between the visual imagination and the destructive imagination of the psychopath" and that the novel "is about the sinisterly thin line between one's sense of one's own id as a dangerous thing and one's capacity for moral action."[1] He has also called the novel "an attempt to examine what is happening to the belief systems of individuals in an age when our relentless practice of applied psychology has kicked the legs out from under our social ethic; in an age when the light of reason, far from burning brightly, is guttering terribly."[2] These explanations, however ambitious they might appear, account for only two aspects of the book's narrative levels. The novel's dominant trope concerns a young man who becomes an apprentice and then a licentiate of the Devil in human form, a mentorship in evil that Self satirically conjoins to the protagonist's career in marketing. Superficially this storyline entails a critique of the materialism and amoral equivocations popularly associated with the 1980s. This aspect of the novel is significant, and Self does indeed focus on the ways that the marketplace manipulates and controls civilian life, operating as a "Fat Controller," but this motif also provides an apt metaphor for his more profound meditation on addiction. At still another level the novel is, like his novella "Cock," an examination of the mind of the writer and his relationship—particularly as an omnipotent manipulator—to his subjects. In her review of the novel, Elizabeth Young remarks on this aspect, noting that the shocking episodes of the book "are relatively mild and its structure seems too complex and deliberate merely to serve some meaningless personal surrealism. It seems more probable that Self is attempting to deal with the precise relationship between the writer and the world; that the book offers a rubric of creativity, with Ian as a blank screen on which is projected a creative psychodrama."[3]

With his narrative strata, shifting perspectives, ambiguities, and interweaving characters, Self continually challenges the reader's sense of fixity, ultimately reinforcing the necessity of maintaining suspended disbelief in his fictional universe. *My Idea of Fun* combines these very elements to depict both subjectively and objectively the psychological instabilities stemming from addiction. Self's extended metaphor of capitalism as a conceit for addiction also submits that dependency need not be confined to narcotics and alcohol but that modern life is one of inexorable avid consumption. Regardless of the source of addiction, chemical or psychological, the consequences remain reasonably consistent, most especially the loss of one's autonomy. Self has remarked of his experiences as a heroin addict that "I was doing things that were against my moral will, not just occasionally, but a lot of the time, on a daily basis. I had the distinct sensation that I was a puppet of an addictive manipulator, that there was a kind of sinister hand which was forcing me in directions that I didn't like."[4] These are the primary issues at stake in his first novel.

My Idea of Fun is partly a loose retelling of James Hogg's *The Private Memoirs and Personal Confessions of a Justified Sinner* (1824), which Self echoes thematically and structurally in his plot involving an impressionable young man who comes under Satanic influence; episodes of fuguelike trances; violence, especially murder and sexual assault; the protagonist's domineering mother; and the bifurcated structure of the novel and its narrative perspectives. There are further similarities between the two novels. Like Hogg, Self combines a fantastic storyline with personal anxieties, but where Hogg draws from his Calvinist upbringing and then his dissatisfaction with the Edinburgh literary elite, Self fictionalizes his years of alcohol and drug addiction. Pointing out a primary distinction between his protagonist and Hogg's, Self has Ian Wharton declare that "this . . . isn't intended as a justification of any kind. I don't need to justify myself, I only want to be understood."[5]

Self divides the novel into two separate books, "The First Person" and "The Third Person," separated by a brief transitional interval. This structure suggests a debt to Hogg's divisions of the "Editor's Narrative"—in which the events are recounted in the third person—and the first-person "Private Memoirs and Confessions of a Sinner." In *My Idea of Fun* the "Intermission" section remains a part of the first-person narration but is a return to the moment and place of telling the story, with Ian in his kitchen as his wife sleeps upstairs. With book 2, Ian, according to the novel's internal logic and narrative premise, remains the narrator but has suddenly detached himself from the events he describes, signifying his loss of autonomy and personal identity as an agent of a man he calls the Fat Controller. Recounting the major events of his life in a warts-and-all manner (as his surname suggests) while sitting at his kitchen table, Ian Wharton moves from personal confession to impersonal description.

Declaring that he "has been subjected to the direct marketing of my very soul," Ian presents himself as an archetype of a contemporary form of masculinity: "You've heard of the rogue male," he says, "I am his modern descendant, the junk male" (157). He mulls over a secondary confession: to inform his wife of his secret life as the Devil's apprentice and to inform her that in all probability the child she is carrying is not Ian's but Satan's, and is in fact a fresh incarnation of the Devil. At the outset Ian disingenuously claims to be uncertain about informing his wife, Jane, of these facts and considers suicide instead. He claims in the prologue that he will rely on the reader, his silent confessor, to help him make the proper decision; this is, however, only a ploy to have a sounding board for his story. As with the novel, Ian's identity is heavily layered. His "multi-ply selves" (3)—Ian's "rotten selves" that constitute his "worm's-cast identity, a vermiculation of the very soul" (6)—are revealed gradually and are at times hidden from himself. In the prologue Ian has full knowledge of his "outrages," his euphemism for the orgy of psychopathic violence that he calls his idea of fun, but in the first half of the novel he recalls events from a naïve perspective. The method is to ask the reader to forego judging him morally and to understand his unusual predicament, to offer empathy if not sympathy.

For his part Ian is precluded from experiencing sympathy. After asking the reader to look up "empathy" and "sympathy" in a dictionary, he remarks that "I think you'll find that you've got them the wrong way round, that what you thought was empathy was really sympathy and vice versa. You see, that's been my problem—all the time I thought I was sympathising I was really empathising. I'm not going to make big claims about this semantic quirk but I do think it's worth remarking on, for when two key terms tumble over one another in this fashion you can be sure that something is afoot" (12). What is happening is that the ability to feel has become an ineffectual hybrid of sympathy and empathy, a thwarted synthesis that allows for no feeling beyond one's own pleasures. Ian's transformation from a relative innocent into a callous murderer, torturer, and rapist—a change that coincides with his education and professional growth as a marketing executive—shows the degrees to which he has completely subsumed into his own psyche the desire for selfish pleasure held by his own "determinants," the three individuals he holds responsible for this change in him. These "determinants" shape his perceptions and consciousness. At the beginning of the novel, Ian calls consciousness "a wild primeval place, a realm of the id, where the very manifold of your identity can be gashed open, sundered, so that all the little reflex actions that you call your 'self' will spill out" (15).

Whereas the events in most people's lives are influenced by arbitrary decisions or fate, Ian claims, he holds an unusual position. "I can actually point to my determinants, I can name them even: The Fat Controller for one, Dr Gyggle for two, and if I were pressed for a third it would have to be Mummy" (11). This trio has shaped and scarred Ian's consciousness, and he has at various times embraced and attempted to reject each of them. Notably absent from this brief roster, and from Ian's life since Ian was eleven, is his father, whom the Fat Controller knew in the 1960s and refers to as a "contemptible Essene." The senior Wharton, Ian learns, was among the most successful marketing experts in London and headed his own company, Wharton Marketing, until succumbing to "a fatal kind of ennui" (22). After a few years of prolonged apathy, he vanished from home and never returned. As Ian entered adolescence he was left without a father figure, finding a surrogate in the guise of the mysterious Mr. Broadhurst who for several years resided during the off-season in the caravan park that Ian's mother ran on the Sussex coast.

Throughout the course of *My Idea of Fun,* Broadhurst goes by several distinct identities. As Samuel Northcliffe, he is a wealthy businessman linked to multiple corporate mergers and other aspects of the financial market. When as a teenager Ian receives an unorthodox tutelage from Broadhurst, he begins to refer—at Broadhurst's insistence—to the elder man as The Fat Controller, taking care to capitalize the definite article in speech and thought. This moniker derives from Broadhurst's physical and occasional sartorial resemblance to Sir Topham Hatt in the Rev. W. V. Awdry's popular *Thomas the Tank Engine* series of children's books. Just as Ian's mother thrusts him as a child onto the Island of Sodor as she introduces him to the series, she is also responsible for forcing the fictional character's evil doppelgänger on to Ian. This identity is important to understanding the Fat Controller's implications in the novel. He functions both as a puppeteer controlling human agency—a malevolent forerunner of the governing octet in "Between the Conceits" from *Grey Area*—and a corruptor of innocence. The Island of Sodor foreshadows the Land of Children's Jokes in the last half of *My Idea of Fun* by representing the innocence that Ian loses, even if he has only a precarious innocence in childhood.[6]

The Fat Controller's actual identity is the Devil, and his relationship to Ian quickly becomes quasi-paternal. As Ian's mentor the Fat Controller helps him to master his gift of eidetic memory—a form of photographic memory and a trait that, in keeping with Self's tendency in the novel to imbue his characters with characteristics similar to members of his own family, Ian shares with Self's paternal grandfather[7]—and introduces Ian to a phenomenon the Fat Controller terms "retroscendence," the ability to literally visualize in multiple dimensions the history of a product from its origin to point of sale. A similar mentorship occurs in Hogg's *Confessions of a Justified Sinner*, in which the protagonist, Robert Wringhim, meets a man who identifies himself as "Gil-Martin" but turns out to be Satan. Playing upon Wringhim's Calvinist upbringing and hatred for his brother and biological father, Gil-Martin convinces Wringhim that the elect are above human laws and the two begin committing murders. Gil-Martin has the ability to assume the shape of anyone he wishes after observing them for a period, and he becomes Wringhim's shadowy double, committing legal and moral crimes as Wringhim while the latter lapses into a fugue state. *My Idea of Fun* contains variations on these details, but the most prominent similarity lies in the influence that the Satan figures wield over the impressionable followers. Self extends this personification of evil power to the Freudian id, or primal realm of the psychological unconsciousness, by using it as a representation of addiction.

As Ian becomes a slave to his master, the Fat Controller, his own will is thwarted until his will and the Fat Controller's are one and the same, a hyper-realized construal of the "will to power" concept that the nineteenth-century German philosophers Arthur Schopenhauer and Friedrich Nietzsche posit as a will to life itself. In *Beyond Good and Evil*, Nietzsche clarifies this phrase to convey a view of life as "*essentially* appropriation, injury, overpowering what is alien and weaker; suppression, hardness, imposition of one's own forms, incorporation and at least, at its mildest, exploitation."[8] Ian displays in one manner of action or another each of these elements throughout the novel, becoming increasingly similar to his mentor. As Ian reflects on "Broadhurst's Wager," "the correct way round of looking" at theology (162), he remarks that "there's no fun anymore, just my idea of it. Mine and his, his and mine" (163). In the typical Faust story the protagonist enters into a form of commerce with Satan, exchanging his eternal soul for material or intellectual rewards. While Ian does indeed profit from the knowledge that the Fat Controller doles out to him over a period of years, he appears to have been the commodity in his mother's own Satanic covenant.

Her "maternal complicity" (64) originates from the 1960s, either from when Ian was an infant or prior to his birth. Because Samuel Northcliffe knew the senior Wharton during this period, there is a suggestion that she agreed to make her son the Fat Controller's apprentice upon the boy's coming of age in order to satisfy her own desire for social elevation. Ian surmises that the Fat Controller's interest in him is literally rather than figuratively paternal. After remarking that it is difficult for him to discuss his mother while she is still alive, Ian claims that for the moment "I can only think of her as an assisting adept, a distaff manipulator. It was she who set it up between me and The Fat Controller. I have long suspected that they may have been lovers at some time or other. . . . This matter of the potential relationship between The Fat Controller and my mother is of some importance . . . and were I intent on constructing a defence for myself its actuality might well be at the core" (24). Nearly every aspect of her personality resurfaces during Ian's adulthood.

During a period following the Fat Controller's departure from Cliff Top, the caravan park and bed-and-breakfast that Ian's mother owns in Saltdean, Ian begins to consider the possibility that he might have "been the victim of an extended delusion" involving Broadhurst as a way of compensating for the lack of a male role model in his life: "Perhaps I wasn't the plaything of a mage, who was determined to drag me into a frightening and chaotic world of naked will, only a seriously neurotic person in need of help" (125). His combined neuroses, most especially a generalized sense of fear as well as sexual frustration, take their toll on Ian's academic performance at Sussex University, and his tutor, concerned with Ian's mental health, makes an appointment for him with the university counselor. Reminiscent of both Self's recurring character Zack Busner and William Burroughs's Dr. Benway from *The Naked Lunch*, Hieronymous Gyggle constitutes an integral aspect of the manipulative trinity in Ian's life. A psychiatrist with unorthodox clinical methods and dubious ethics, Gyggle initially works as a counselor at Ian's university. Gyggle confirms that Ian suffers from a complex delusion and quickly proves to him that Ian's gift for visualization is a manifestation of his delusions. He further diagnoses Ian as "a borderline personality, with pronounced schizoid tendencies" (139), replicating a psychiatrist's diagnosis of the nineteen-year-old Self when he was already a confirmed heroin addict. Self has attributed his own diagnosis to the mimetic nature of addiction, and borderline personality disorder is frequently associated with substance abuse. Although Ian exhibits symptoms of both disorders, his behavior stems from the Fat Controller's influence on Ian as an adolescent and adult.

As Ian moves from Sussex to London to begin his new job as a marketing assistant for an oil valves manufacturer, I. A. Wartberg Limited, Gyggle accepts a consultancy in London. Gyggle heads the hospital's drug dependency unit and sees the heroin addicts in his care as "research fodder" (145), and in league with the Fat Controller he uses them to stage elaborate nightmare scenarios as he supposedly subjects Ian to deep sleep therapy. This follows an initial treatment of sensory deprivation where Gyggle places Ian in a sensory deprivation tank he has installed in the hospital's basement. As Ian prepares to voyage into "inner space" (149), he is distracted by the quotidian sounds of the external world. Rather than a failed therapy, this experience becomes a calculated preparation for Ian's deep sleep treatments and their concomitant nightmarish visions, which Ian later learns are in fact "heroin-induced hypnogogia" (297). These dreams ostensibly occur in a realm Ian calls the Land of Children's Jokes, which distorts childish play into a world of violent and scatological grotesque horror through the vivified personifications of puerile riddles.

A place of gross and violent deformity, where allusions to nursery rhymes extrapolate the fables' sinister characteristics, the Land of Children's Jokes suggests to Ian that few things are as innocent as they might have once seemed. During the first section of the novel Ian believes that Gyggle is genuinely helping to cure him of his supposed delusions, but in the second half he learns that Gyggle has been serving as one of the Fat Controller's minions. As Colin MacCabe notes of the novel's ending, the "simple elision of the two worlds of money and the unconscious, the partnership of Gyggle and the Fat Controller, reveals to Ian Wharton that he is in fact a psychopathic monster."[8] Like Zack Busner, Gyggle is an arrogant lord of his psychiatric realm who uses his patients and colleagues to facilitate his own professional advancement. Where Busner has had his Concept House and the wards at Heath Hospital, Gyggle acquires his own sections of the Lurie Foundation Hospital for Dipsomaniacs where he subverts ethical standards, moral obligations, and legal proscriptions. Rather than treating Ian, Gyggle aids the Fat Controller by making Ian dependent upon both men as he loses the remaining vestiges of his own will.

Self has said that it is "a hard furrow to plow, writing fiction in this way—off the back of my drug addiction," adding that writing itself "can be a kind of addiction too."[9] In *My Idea of Fun,* Ian Wharton's tangled psychiatric state and cognitive perceptions fuse the creative aspects of writing and the destructive nature of addiction into a multiflorous metaphor. The novel could be interpreted fairly as depicting either of these topics—in addition to others such as materialism and as a surreal apologia for Self's life—but one of Self's strengths is his ability to weave them into a cohesive entity. Ian claims that his "painfully acquired powers of description" (4) fail to do justice in rendering the experiences he relates, most predominantly his peculiar form of enhanced visualization, but he describes his eidetic reveries in effective detail. Moreover, the surreal qualities of his eidetic visions evoke a novelist's imagination and narcotic effects.

Ian's eidetic memory consists of "internal images that have the full force of conventional vision" (15), an extraordinarily detailed form of photographic memory frequently found in autistics. His abilities extend to near microscopic detail and allow him to visualize in various dimensions, a manifestation that Gyggle tells him is simply a delusion. The Fat Controller supplements Ian's eidesis through a visual journey of "retroscendence," a neologism that the Fat Controller coins (108). Through retroscendence, Ian witnesses "The History of the Product" (117), covering all aspects of the production of his underpants from the cotton fields of the Egyptian Delta to their ultimate place of sale as a manufactured and labeled product at a fashionable men's wear shop on Chelsea's King's Road. During this virtual history tour Ian becomes a silent spectator to the dire life of the El Azain, the laborers in the cotton fields, to the hazardous processes of converting the cotton into fabric, to the haggling of a London cotton broker, culminating in the design and sale of Ian's shorts. This "global network of industry" (113) reveals the human toil and physical and emotional costs involved in creating even the most commonplace garments, which in this case are sold at inflated prices at a high-end boutique where the label carries more value than the actual product. Although this "History of the Product" vision is on one level an imaginative indictment on material consumption at the expense of unseen human suffering, it also closely parallels the production of narcotics. Not simply an exercise in displaying the novelist's abilities of exterior representation, this bizarre eidetic journey becomes something of a cipher for the interior workings of the addict's consciousness and the protracted swath that his persistent desire carves across the globe.

Although *My Idea of Fun* received a fair amount of positive— even glowing—notices, many reviewers focused on the more sensational aspects of the novel. Unmistakably *My Idea of Fun* contains scenes of extraordinary violence, most notably Ian's "outrages" involving the torture and killing of Fucker Finch's pit bull—although he appears only by name in *My Idea of Fun*, Gary "Fucker" Finch becomes an important character in *The Book of Dave* (2006)—and the decapitation and necrophiliac assault on a homeless man aboard an underground train. Self has said, perhaps disingenuously, that the former episode was the result of his narrative mischief, his desire "to wind people up."[10] The *Sunday Times* review places such scenes in a neutral context, observing that "while there are only a few scenes of X-rated atrocities within the book, one feels throughout a distinct horripilation, a quavering anticipation of something about to spring on us over the next page. It is a book you tend to read through your fingers."[11] Taking a more negative view, the *TLS* review of the novel remarks that such episodes suggest an authorial prurience that diminishes Self's more legitimate strengths as a writer: "there is something of the unpleasant adolescent boy about [these scenes]. For all his cleverness and sickness, though,

Self is still an exhilaratingly sharp and fluent writer. His almost excessively articulate focus on the scuzziness of life has already been compared with Martin Amis, and it is only his idiosyncracies—for philosophy tutorials from Hell and for pulling the wings off flies—that condemn him to be a more marginal figure."[12] The reviewer for London's *Guardian* takes a less reasoned view of the book's violent scenes, asserting that they result from literary competition: "Will Self is so occupied with showing off how much nastier he can be than anyone else that he forgets to animate the fear and the hate, or to add the single drop of humanity."[13] Yet for a writer who has expressed his lack of interest in developing realistic characters, Self imbues Ian Wharton with a sense of humanity, which Wharton annuls at the end of the novel.

Even though Ian's mother is the most significant female figure in his life, her role appears primarily to give birth to Ian and then to prepare him for The Fat Controller's arrival, functioning as a vessel for this self-styled Brahmin of the Banal's propagation. Two other women play vital roles in allowing Ian to seem more of a realistic adult male than he previously had done, and then they function largely as inverse foils against which the dark depths of Ian's psychotic proclivities become apparent. Not coincidentally, both women are nominally similar.

June Richards is one of Ian's fellow students at Sussex University, an apparently likeminded conservative sharing his marketing major. Tim Hargreaves—the tutor who introduces Ian to Gyggle, thus positing the likelihood that Hargreaves too has fallen under the influence of the Fat Controller—facilitates their meeting by suggesting that June borrow Ian's copiously detailed and precise notes. June and Ian go to a film and dinner in Brighton,[14] replicating certain of Ian's experiences with the Fat

Controller, and as they stand outside the Metropole Hotel he experiences his first brush with sexual contact (100). Following the Fat Controller's intervention as Ian begins to penetrate June's body and the realm of the sexually initiated, when Ian sees her at the university he becomes aloof and remote, passively ending the relationship. At one point, he is startled by the hostility she displays toward him, but the reason for this becomes clear in the closing pages of the novel: "I had happily joined him in mesmerising, drugging and then sexually assaulting poor June in my caravan. There was no mystery now as to why she could never bear to talk to me again. Despite being unconscious throughout, some ghostly memory of the experience must have stayed with her" (290–91). With the Fat Controller leading the way, resulting in yet another "outrage" from this sinister mentorship, he and Ian become binary incubi as they rape the insensible June. In a seemingly fortuitous coincidence June is not the only one who retains "some ghostly memory" of this trauma.

During an expository flashback in the "Land of Children's Jokes" chapter, Jane Carter, Ian's future wife, buys a toy figurine of the Fat Controller for her elder brother, who ungraciously rejects the gift. The toy begins to represent for her humiliation and eventually she associates the figure with an ominous masculine presence, one that follows her through puberty. At thirteen she identifies "the presence for what it so clearly was, the Dionysian other, Pan, Priapus" (193). Following her first sexual experience years later, she has a nightmare in which this presence sucks at her vagina "with the mechanical insensitivity of a domestic appliance" as she lies silent and helpless (194). The dream deeply traumatizes Jane, causing her to feel "sexually constrained by something that lay outside herself" (194) and instilling in her a phobia of cunnilingus. This visionary experience—a kind of prescendence rather than retroscendence—links Jane with June Richards but also foretells one of Ian's final outrages in the book's closing pages.

Names in Self's fiction carry connotative significance; "Jane" typically signifies a safe and bland middle-class identity, an English Everywoman to the Everyman of "Dave." In a fit of neurotic pity Jane Carter recognizes her conformist identity, feeling "herself to be just one amongst a multitude of Janes. . . . They all looked the same, they all faced in the same direction and they all threw up their arms. They formed the most highly dispersed Busby Berkeley–style chorus line ever—this phantom army of high-kicking Janes" (236). Such titular associations extend to innocent vulnerability as Jane and her nominal near-twin June fall victim to Ian's psychopathic assaults. Both attacks are hyperbolic depictions of an addict's difficulty in forming stable relationships when drug dependency is accompanied by borderline personality disorder, which entails a thwarting of affect. Ian and Jane's marriage fulfills the Fat Controller's "elective affinity." To signify his sanctioning of their union, and in the process gaining for Ian the approval of Jane's parents, Samuel Northcliffe stands as Ian's best man at their wedding. Throughout *My Idea of Fun* the chapter headings divulge each respective chapter's concentration on a key theme, but no chapter heading carries the same descriptive (and allusive) significance as the one in which Ian and Jane marry: "The North London Book of the Dead (Reprise)."

This title evokes a connection to the lead story in *The Quantity Theory of Insanity,* but it also contains a Janus aspect of simultaneously looking ahead to *How the Dead Live* in that it provides an idiosyncratic variation on the *Tibetan Book of the Dead.* Near the end of the chapter, Ian watches as Gyggle's collection of junkies engage in a litany of commercial brand names, all of which have attained the status of generic products, in order to prepare the soul of a dying addict for its journey into the afterlife that in *My Idea of Fun* becomes a transition into sheer materiality. This occurs in one room of the hospital as Ian's fellow marketeers are gathered in an adjoining room that serves as their office, emphasizing one of the novel's central motifs—that as disparate as the heroin addicts and marketing executives might initially seem "fundamentally they're all engaged in the same activity" (297). Likewise, the scene reflects Ian's divided personality as a self-described "junk male" who embodies both worlds.

In this crucial chapter, which returns to the first-person point of view to demonstrate Ian's new if ambiguous self-awareness, Ian experiences a series of revelations that transform him utterly. He realizes that he has instigated his mentorship with the Fat Controller and that he submerged key truths deep inside his memory. He recounts his outrages beginning with the murder of a woman at a theater in Brighton—a crime that, initially attributed to the Fat Controller, suggests a link to the assassination in London of the Bulgarian dissident Georgi Markov in 1977—and continuing into acts of escalating violence and sensationalism. A culminating attack, unlike the others not previously depicted, reveals the inherent self-awareness that Self inscribes into the novel. Ian performs an act of literal textual violence, using a large-print library book to beat an elderly woman to death (291). As Ian declares that he has always held "a sense of being in the now, of a kind of alienation from history itself" (291), Self subversively equates Ian's blocked affect and temporal estrangement with the voyeuristic qualities of fiction, making the reader complicit in treating the book's violence as a kind of psychopathic pornography.

Ian's assertion of willingness to allow for audience participation (11) finally acquires fuller credence in this dark realization of communal involvement. He has elsewhere insisted on similarity between the audience and the storyteller by including the reader in his narrative, dividing them into two camps of addiction that replicate the inherent nature of writing and reading of fiction: "We're like coke heads or chronic masturbators, aren't we? Attempting to crank the last iota of abandonment out of an intrinsically empty and mechanical experience" (163). One implication is that the reader must then wrestle with Self's manipulation of his narrative audience, his destabilizing the reader's moral will by presenting scenes in which the reader indulges. Further, Ian removes himself from moral censure by comparing himself to his mentor: "I held myself to be beyond all morality, a towering superman whose activities could not even be observed from the grovelling positions of mere mortals, let alone judged. Yet it also remained perfectly plausible for me to deny that I had done any of these awful things at all" (291–92). This passage echoes the situation that Hogg places his Robert Wringhim in, an allusion that Self soon makes explicit as Ian comments on his "delightfully separate centres of self": "when they commingled fully there was a sweet melancholia engendered alongside the terror of the dark and the arrogance of the justified sinner" (292–93).

Whether as Broadhurst, Northcliffe, or any of his other adopted identities, the Fat Controller remains the dominant presence in Ian's life. He comprehensively disrupts and distorts all potentially meaningful relationships in Ian's life, precluding Ian's ability to sympathize with others, and comprehensively pollutes the conventional father-son relationship. Indeed the Fat Controller is reborn through a final outrage that remains off the page: Ian's actualizing of Jane's nightmarish abortion from which Ian becomes the apparent father to the Fat Controller. As Ian leaves London for New York City to work on a new marketing campaign, it seems likely that his psychopathic behavior will continue, unhampered by any residual moral conscience.

With the novel's open-ended epilogue, Self implies that there is no tidy resolution to Ian's life and that his condition will remain much as it was previously, with Ian continuing his violent ways. All along, the novel steers the reader toward this understanding. Self utilizes a pattern of constructive repetitions to emphasize particular words and motifs, and the novel's bifurcated structure serves as an emblem for these internal reflections as events are narrated through two perspectives. In this regard Self uses the book's two primary divisions as a distorted mirror to reflect and alter one another, making experiences and characters simultaneously similar and distinct much in the way that his fictional world reflects the real world. An important pair of reflective schemes epitomize the metafictional plane of *My Idea of Fun* and can be regarded as a muted formulation of Self's narrative attitude toward destabilizing fictional realism.

As *My Idea of Fun* effects the transition in narrative perspective at the end of its intermission, in which the third-person narrator asserts his own lack of objectivity, Ian is transformed from specific subject to a kind of generic entity, a narrative plaything. Where Ian had previously become the narrative subject for the case study on his eidetic gifts in a paper that Bateson, the clinical psychologist who prefigures Gyggle at Ian's primary school, publishes in a professional journal (49), and Gyggle as well had mulled the possibility of similarly publishing an account of his supposed treatments of Ian, Self comprehensively strips Ian of autonomy: "And now, Ian Wharton, now that you are no longer the subject of this cautionary tale, merely its object, now that you are just another unproductive atom staring out from the windows of a branded monad, now that I've got you where I want you, let the wild rumpus begin" (165). Ian's "wild rumpus," his spree of violent "outrages" that include the decapitation of and subsequent sexual assault on the homeless man or "dosser" on board a London underground train, finds its equivalent in a short story that appeared several months before the publication of *My Idea of Fun.*

"World of Serial" describes a contemporary society in which transgressive behavior stems from the abstention from violence as well as selfless actions. An example of satirical inversion, the story upends commonly held views on social etiquette and crime. Although it opens with a prosaic scene of domestic realism, "World of Serial" quickly introduces its twist on social and moral codes with a news report of police failing to discover any corpses on the premises of a Warwickshire house. Citizens routinely engage in serial murder, and as the protagonist calmly reflects after dispatching a family on the roadway, the murder formed "one of the neatest multiple killings of his life."[15] Another character garrotes a pair of Tube guards with a length of cheese-wire (32), a double homicide that has a kinship to various killings by Ian Wharton and the Fat Controller. Notably, the police pride themselves on their facility with violence, intimidating suspects, and forging evidence. In fact refraining from such acts is regarded as not only shameful but criminal.

One man is sentenced to a life term in prison for "not raping his 15-month old daughter" (32), a "non-event" that foreshadows the shame attached to the lack of familial sex in *Great Apes.* The Warwickshire police establish a "non-event room" at their headquarters to contend with the problem of a physically anonymous suspect on the loose whose shocking crime is that he "isn't remotely dangerous" (32). By presenting inaction as criminal and scandalous, Self depicts a society that appears to be struggling against a tendency toward indolence and monotony, what Ian Wharton calls "a fatal kind of ennui." This is one key element of Self's satirical target, it seems, exposing the ways that people attempt to thwart what might be a habitual drive toward inertia. Self further examines this idea of what he has expressed as "a future of boredom, a Switzerland of the soul,"[16] in *Grey Area*.

CHAPTER FIVE

The Death of Affect

Grey Area and Other Stories

By the time Will Self published *Grey Area* in 1994, he had quickly amassed a body of work with which critics could gauge his development as a writer, and the book appeared in the wake of heavy publicity concerning his work and life. Critics took note, but for the most part they confined their reviews to the work itself. In his review of the collection for London's *Sunday Times,* Peter Kemp name-checks each of Self's previous books and includes the seemingly obligatory comparison to Martin Amis while also seeing an intentional design in the parallels of Self's name and the ideas he explores in his fiction. Kemp sees in Self's work a form of nominal reflection, a "narcissism" that emerges thematically throughout the collection. "Ever since his first book," Kemp remarks, "his fiction has enjoyed playing with the concepts of free will and loss of self. In his fantastic scenarios, people are reduced to zombies ruled by eerie forces or deprived of their identity by outre happenings."[1]

Will Eaves likewise opens his approving *TLS* review by show-ing how the collection relates to its predecessor. Eaves observes that similarities between the two collections indicate Self's narra-tive method and his satirical objects: "The main targets, as in his first book, *The Quantity Theory of Insanity* (1991), are psy-chotherapy and pseudoscience and, as before, the satirical motor is cranked up by narrators, witnesses and correspondents who fail to extricate themselves from the lunacy they have been trained to diagnose and control."[2] For Eaves, Self's narrative technique provides an identifier, remarking that "Self's trademark is his marrying of cod-philosophy to provincial frustration." The close attention these reviewers place on his work, assessing its themes and fictional methods, suggests that while Self might in fact be a "creature of the media"[3] with the publication of *Grey Area* he had established his legitimacy as a significant writer, one whose work merited methodical consideration. Moreover, through their efforts to connect some of the various narrative strands in his fiction critics implicitly acknowledged the self-referential and continuous nature of the work itself, with its multitude of detours and roundabouts.

As Kemp and Thomas Mallon[4] have commented, Self's stories frequently concern issues of control and its loss. Self explores a condition of psychological entropy—the gray areas that permeate this volume, an expression of intellectual and emotional inertia with its roots branching out to J. G. Ballard's concept of the "death of affect," that is "a demise of feeling an emotion."[5] Like Ballard, most especially in his novel *Crash* and his anti-novel *The Atrocity Exhibition,* Self depicts a society on the verge of psychic apocalypse as technology and deracination thwart essential human emotions. His characters exist in a virtual Newton's cradle, propelled to collide incessantly and cacophonously with one another until they succumb to a loss of momentum. In *My Idea of Fun,* the Fat Controller observes the citizens of London going about their lives, noting that they "are in transit from some urban *Heimat,* an ur-suburb, a grey area. They are like colonists who have set out *en masse,* lemminglike, uncomprehending, obeying an instinctive need to buy a newspaper in another country."[6] Continuing this idea, *Grey Area* presents an image of contemporary England where its inhabitants reel lugubriously from their invisible tethers; the stories chart this process of winding down and its physical and psychological ramifications. "Between the Conceits," the first story in the book, posits this motif as it puns on the semantic connotations of its title.

"Conceit" suggests the arrogance of the narrator, and it also implies the story's central metaphor concerning social power and subjection. The narrator's binary topics are control and social hierarchy, through which Self satirizes the continued presence of the British class system. "Between the Conceits" takes the form of a confession as the narrator imposes on his audience the presumed facts he sets out during the course of his narration, a sequence of supposed revelations occasioned by a conversation in a pub.[7] A modern day Ancient Mariner of sorts, the narrator unburdens himself at the expense of his audience, insisting on an "intimacy" with his listener (8). Despite his contentions that he is engaging the listener/reader in conversation (7–8, 18), the narration remains a monologue. His audience's reactions are not only presumed but actually included in his narrative, most prominently through the narrator's abrupt objections and interruptions which impart the illusion of dialogue.

Modern narrators, especially in the first-person voice, manifest a high degree of dubious veracity, undermining their narrative authority. The narrator of this story presents a conundrum regarding how the readers should view his preposterous claim that he is one of "only eight people in London" (3)—that is, one member of an octet that directs the lives of all Londoners, and appears as a mixture of legendary mystical and secret elites such as the Rosicrucians and the Talmudic Lamed-Vav Nistarim, the anonymous thirty-six righteous men who carry as their burden the sins and sorrows of the world in order to prevent its destruction. In addition to the narrator—a middle-aged, former bookstore clerk[8] who lives with his octogenarian, bedridden mother (16)—this dysfunctional cabal consists of seven men and women charged with controlling the fate of their assigned proportion of London residents. Each of these eight people exhibit varying motivations in how they manipulate the lives of their charges, typically through banal events. These characters reportedly act respectively from "capriciousness," "some perverted religiosity," a longing "to see everything," a "desire for orderliness,"and from having "everyone's best intentions at heart," while the narrator claims to act from "absolute probity" (16–17). But the narrator's actions, if they are to be credited, reveal his own impulsive behavior: "I stretch, then relax—and 35,665 white-collar workers leave their houses a teensy bit early for work" (9).

Just as the narrator refuses to admit a uniform equality among his elite group of custodians, he is even more condescending toward those whose lives he purportedly controls, fantasizing about his charges' metaphysical deception to divert himself from his own bouts of depression: "When I'm really down it amuses me to toy with this notion: that one of the little people might discover the truth. Discover not only that their freedom is a delusion; but that, furthermore, instead of being the hapless tool of some great deity, shoved up on a towering Titian-type cloud, they are instead jerked this way and that by a pervert in Bloomsbury, or a dullard in the Shell Centre, or an old incontinent in Clapton. Ye-es, it would be droll" (17–18). Self presents three main possibilities regarding the narrator's reliability: that he is delusional, intoxicated, or sincere; these possibilities are not mutually exclusive. In allowing these interpretive options, Self modestly realigns the balance of power between author and reader, but in order to unravel this knot of narrative implications the reader must explore the fissures that exist between the lines or conceits of the work itself, as the story's title implies.

Elsewhere in *Grey Area,* Self experiments with his narrative personae, using his first-person narrators to break from the normal expectations readers might have about a male author. As in "Between the Conceits," when using the first-person Self prefers to withhold the narrator's name, a method that creates a sense of pervasive anonymity and suits the tenor of the collection aptly. When the narrator reveals her or his identity, as with Wayne Fein in "The Indian Mutiny," Self addresses the very issue of public personality. "The Indian Mutiny" satirizes media personalities through the confession of Fein, host of a chat show entitled *Fein Time Tonight,* who as an adult remains haunted by his typical juvenile behavior at school. This culminates in Fein's recollection of a dream involving his former history teacher, Mr. Vello, who breaks into sobs before the narrator's vampiric assault on him (31). In this dream Fein expresses a triptych of submerged guilt: for his adolescent insolence toward his teacher, for exploiting guests on his television program, and for the injustices the British empire visited upon India. Vello appears as an analogue of the strict Latin teacher Self had during his fifth form at Christ's College, Finchley, a "man who represented everything I hated . . . but I came to like him and he came to like me."[9] Three stories in *Grey Area*—"A Short History of the English Novel," "Grey Area," and "The End of the Relationship—contain female narrators, returning to Self's interest in gender identity.

Of these three narrators only Geraldine in "A Short History of the English Novel" is identified, but even this name functions as a complement to her publishing friend, Gerard. The story itself is a sustained joke on the idea that all waiters are actually aspiring writers, and as Geraldine and Gerard visit restaurants and cafés they encounter a stream of frustrated novelists. Another journey through London and its suburbs occurs in the book's concluding story, "The End of the Relationship." Called an "emotional Typhoid Mary" (282) by her boyfriend, the narrator unwittingly disrupts the emotional stability of everyone around her. "Perhaps all this awful mismatching, this emotional grating, these Mexican stand-offs of trust and commitment, were somehow in the air," she muses at a restaurant following a decisive fight with her boyfriend and observing another woman in an analogous situation. "It was a contagion that was getting to all of us; a germ of insecurity that had lodged in our breasts and was now fissioning frantically, creating a domino effect as relationship after relationship collapsed in a rubble of mistrust and acrimony" (259). Her boyfriend makes a similar observation, placing the narrator at the center of this angst-laden outbreak: "You've got some kind of bacillus inside you, a contagion —everything you touch you turn to neurotic ashes with your pick-pick-picking away at the fabric of people's relationships" (282). The narrator's infectious bleak karma, which sends emotional shockwaves to weaken or wreck the marriages of every couple in the story, depicts an environment that is more grimly homogeneous than its inhabitants suspect.

"Grey Area" presents a comparable crisis, one in which all of London has fallen victim to a peculiar malaise. In this story the unnamed narrator has arranged her life around a series of trivial rituals at home and at her office, and these quotidian routines provide her with a distraction from the bland inertia of her life. Displaying characteristics of Obsessive-Compulsive Disorder she inflates the importance of methodical placement (171). With such fervent devotion to regularity, the disruption of her otherwise predictable menstrual cycle leads to a moment of slight yet epiphanic clarity, that nothing had changed for six weeks (176).

Superficially "Grey Area" is a witty if conventional satire on the tedium of office routines, drawing attention to the obvious targets: unvarying workloads; the exaggerated importance of the company, manifested through the quasi-personification of corporate divisions and titles such as Department, Company, and Head of Company (168); an environment that demands allegiance to format and protocol, creating an atmosphere of institutional sterility; even variations on sexual politics and office flirtations. The design of the first edition of *Grey Area* seems to advocate this reading. Issued in two formats, in hardcover with illustrated boards and in a spiralbound softcover format that replicates an office manual, the book's cover features a photograph of a minimalist office workstation, an impersonal gray and beige environment broken only by a lone plant beside an opaque window and a red chair rising above an intersection of dim shadows. But the eponymous "grey area" is more than physical space, transcending the geographical boundaries of office and city; it literally and figuratively encompasses the brain as well. Self frequently examines the syncretism, or union of typically opposite principles or factions, of physical and psychic spaces—hence the centrality of London in *The Quantity Theory of Insanity* and the M40 corridor in *Grey Area*—and in "Grey Area" they meld into an account of ubiquitous ennui.

Whereas "Between the Conceits" ascribes identities to the forces controlling the urban population, "Grey Area" proffers a weeks-long stasis with no foreseeable end. Like the narrator's ceaseless commitment to tidying her desk and other rituals of minutiae, any trivial action suddenly acquires significance. "How small does an event have to be before it ceases to be an event," the narrator asks (173), a question Zack Busner poses as well during his cameo near the story's conclusion (197). A modification of the interrogatives in Bob Dylan's 1960s anthem "Blowin' in the Wind," this question points out how the mundane becomes engrossing in a society that is beginning to confront its static character (198). Self presents an image of a London that has shed the vestiges of its inimitability, creating an effect of perpetual dreariness. By atomizing the story's setting and action—chiseling away to form a series of concentric microcosms—he satirizes the fluid ease with which parochial concerns can become collective ones, entailing a loss of individualism as a result. His narrator's unyielding fascination with order and miniaturization, a totalizing obsession with the trivial, demonstrates the ease with which humans are toyed with and manipulated in Self's fiction. He illustrates this point by having his narrator discover in her former boss's former office a Newton's cradle that features, in lieu of ball bearings, "tiny, humanoid figures hanging from the threads by their tiny aluminum hands" (194). Such indications of their absence of autonomous will reminds Self's characters that it is he who orders their universe, a fact that a few characters obstinately refuse to accept.

Busner's appearance in the story links "Grey Area" to "Inclusion®" while also augmenting Busner's fictional ubiquity. Displaying his characteristic habit of rolling and unrolling his ever-present mohair tie (195), Busner and another "pop academic," Professor Stein,[10] appear on the BBC program *Newsnight* to debate the implications of the social stasis; in keeping with the tenor of the story and its sequence of nonevents, they reach no conclusion. Indeed, the social inertia provides merely a pretext for the performances of Busner and Stein mediated by Peter Snow, the show's actual presenter for several years. Television becomes the perfect medium to display personality over substance, and the anticlimactic result of this particular broadcast accentuates the willingness of viewers to become enthralled by inconsequential concerns. "Inclusion®" continues this idea but with a crucial variation: rather than a symptom of an under-lying condition, or the social malady itself, it is the consequence of a supposed remedy.

"Inclusion®" is notable for several reasons, including its dense narrative layering, its continuation of Busner's story, its introduction of Simon Dykes's madness that provides the hidden back story for *Great Apes,* and its attack on the pharmaceutical industry's contemporary eminence. The story teems with subtle allusions, with referents ranging from Self's previous fiction to Maurice Maeterlinck and William Burroughs. "Inclusion®" contains the most complex narrative strata of any of Self's short stories, presenting an invisible first-person narrator who displays the apparently objective qualities of third person. This implied author addresses the reader directly, temporarily removing the veil of disbelief in order to foreground the reading process itself. The story embeds three separate documents of which the story's principal narrator is the de facto editor, a postmodern variation of the epistolary method.

Purporting to be a found document that, like a series of Russian nesting dolls, opens up to reveal a marketing brochure, a dairy receipt, and four subsumed texts, the story challenges conventional ideas of authorship and originality. Indeed Self includes an explanatory "author's note" that temporarily dis-solves the distinction between author and narrator (203); it remains ambiguous as to whether the "authorship" of this foot-note should be ascribed properly to Self as narrator or whether he gives us an anonymous editor-narrator. The narrator walks the reader through the act of opening the folder that contains the information pertaining to Inclusion, an experimental anti-depressant manufactured by Cryborg Pharmaceutical Indus-tries. Tucked inside this folder replete with marketing data is a confidential, word-processed report from the company's senior public relations manager, R. P Hawke, to the corporate board. Self plays with the idea of reading as a voyeuristic act as his narrator addresses the reader: "God, how exciting! . . . You have a prickly little thrill, don't you? You have the thrill of reading someone's private correspondence in a silent house, on a Sunday afternoon" (204). Intensifying this covert voyeurism, Hawke's report includes a direction to the Board of Directors that they destroy the documents to avert a security breach—to prevent furtive readings of these texts.

Themes such as authority and control are central to "Inclusion®" and to Self's fiction in general. In this story it is the illicit nature of Cryborg's pharmaceutical experiments that shows how easily authority, narrative or otherwise, might be abused. At the center of this particular abuse, heightening both the ethical and moral breaches of the offenders' misconduct, is a violation of trust. Busner, Dr. Anthony Bohm, who works as a general practitioner in the Chilterns, and MacLachlan, the local pharmacist, conspire to conduct the illegal testing of the experimental drug Inclusion on unsuspecting subjects, thereby sabotaging the trust of the larger medical community. Although the full consequence of this trial on one of Busner's "guinea-pigs" (204), Simon Dykes, provides the context for Self's second novel, *Great Apes*, "Inclusion®" should not be dismissed as merely a prequel to that novel. Other writers, most prominently Jonathan Coe in *What a Carve Up!*,[11] portray similar violations of trust in the medical establishment—with Coe depicting such failures as a means of satirizing the privatization of the National Health Service under the Thatcher government—but Self's objectives are apparently to show how various agents can collude to obstruct an individual's autonomy. Few things, perhaps, can sap free will as effectively and catastrophically as pharmaceuticals, as Self appreciates.

Given his own problems with substance abuse for more than twenty years, and the notoriety he has received as a heroin addict and chronicler of the underground drug culture, there remains a lingering presumption that Self not only treats drugs lightly in his fiction but that he glamorizes them. In fact he presents drugs in a consistently negative fashion, whether his characters decide for themselves to indulge in narcotics or whether, as in "Inclusion®," pharmaceuticals are administered to them. When he places drugs alongside laws and cultural taboos inveighing against their use, Self attempts to remove narcotics from moral censure, noting the hypocrisy of prohibiting street drugs when alcohol and a plethora of popular antidepressant medications have also demonstrated tragic effects. Citing his own experience, though, Self acknowledges that many readers can misconstrue an author's message when subversive subjects such as narcotics are a writer's focus. Noting the influence of William Burroughs on his own adolescent aspirations to be a writer, Self remarks that his "form prize in the lower sixth at Christ's College, Finchley, was *Naked Lunch*. As far as I was concerned, Burroughs demonstrated that you could have it all: live outside the law, get stoned the whole time, and still be hailed by Norman Mailer as 'the only living American writer conceivably possessed of genius.' When I awoke from this delusion, aged twenty, diagnosed by a psychiatrist as a 'borderline personality,' and with a heroin habit, I was appalled to discover that I wasn't a famous underground writer. Indeed, far from being a writer at all, I was simply underground."[12] A renegade psychiatrist, Busner also feels he has a concession to live beyond legal boundaries. His narcissism and abiding interest enable Busner to rationalize the experiment as beneficial to manic depressives, but he insists that "the only way to justify the unethical character of the trial is for me to break down some of the traditional—and, I believe, artificial—distinctions between the scientist and the supposed objects of his study" (221). Busner's chief interest is in advancing his professional and cultural eminence, a standing that might be enhanced by his radical, outlaw reputation—one akin to Self's youthful impression of Burroughs. That Busner and Hieronymous Gyggle from *My Idea of Fun* share a resemblance to Burroughs's Dr. Benway from *The Naked Lunch* is no slight coincidence.

The experimental drug Inclusion, it transpires, is a derivative of the powdered waste from a South American parasitic bee mite, which a tribe called the Maeterlincki harvests from defunct hives. These details emerge via the field report of a researcher, Clive Sumner, to the Cryborg Research Division. Further increasing the textual layering of the story, Sumner's report contains a marginal comment by Busner (214). The Maeterlincki— the tribe's name and social organization allude to Maurice Maeterlinck's *Life of the Bee*—are given to indolence and apathy, and at one point the tribe "had been beset by an abiding and terrible collective depression, a truly pathological boredom and lack of interest" (216) until it discovered the psychotropic benefits of the bee mite. In fact the Maeterlincki so closely resemble the Ur-Bororo from "Understanding the Ur-Bororo" that they might be two versions of the same group.

Such ligatures between Self's various works reveal his fictional universe to be one of continued self-reference. When Busner ultimately claims that he has been "included" within Simon Dykes's mind, becoming "pure intention, a secondary and immaterial will operating within the Dykes psyche" (248), two elements of Self's narrative bond into a new, more disturbing fictional entity. Self places the onus on the reader to pull back each of the textual strata in order to try to discover the origins of, in this case, psychosis and delusion, and he offers no firm resolution, although he explores the consequences of the Inclusion experiment further in *Great Apes*.

Throughout Self's fiction Busner's characteristics are notably consistent, but Dykes appears in two distinct manifestations in *Grey Area* alone, as well as his radical transformation into a chimpanzee in *Great Apes*. Although both are artists, the Dykes of "Inclusion®" and that of "Chest" inhabit alternate realties, two versions of the Thames Valley. The most apparent difference between these twinned characters is in their nomenclature: "Chest" presents a world where all characters possess double-barreled first names, which they use to indicate familiarity. Male characters are given a hyphenated combination of first name and patronymic, and female characters are called by their first names followed by a hyphenated matronymic. Thus Simon Dykes is denoted as Simon-Arthur Dykes, and his wife becomes Jean-Drusilla Dykes. Such manipulation of names, providing a faint whiff of aristocratic status, helps to underscore Self's depiction of the innate injustices of Britain's enduring class system.

Social class remains a strong topic for British writers in particular, and rather than diminishing over the years its presence influences much of British life, especially those portions dealing with the nation's diversified population base. In "Chest," Self presents a rural England that is only slightly removed from its feudal past, and in the process he manages to fuse this depiction of the British class system with ecological concerns. The story's exposition reveals that for two years the area has been afflicted by lethal sulphur pollution, a fog that has "made everything seem disturbingly post-nuclear, irradiated" (135). Discussing the importance of topography, particularly London's, to his work, Self has recounted how his anticipation of discovering a "bucolic idyll" in the English countryside was met with a crushing reality: "The country was crowded, noisy and polluted. My infant son's asthma got worse. At night the sky was bruised with the massive explosion of halogen, forty miles away to the south."[13] With "Chest," he exacerbates these conditions.

Simon-Arthur Dykes is afflicted with asthma, a nerve condition, and even cancer, and his family members appear in only marginally better condition than he. His wife is an invalid, and he has two sick children. Dykes is aware of the irony of living in the country; like Self, he moved his family from London because of his son's asthma, which their London doctor attributed to pollution, but some "four months after they had taken up residence in the Brown House the fog moved in with them" (162). Moreover, the sidewalks outside a newsagent's are covered with splotches of infective sputum, and a young boy carries with him a mask attached to an oxygen cylinder which he shares with his friends and, after some brief prompting, with Dykes. Such democratization, however, does not transfer to the adult world. Instead, snobbery and pride override the charitable instincts of the children. When Dykes invites Dave-Dave Hutchinson, the manager of Marten's, the newsagent's, to his house, Hutchinson is subjected to the snobbery of Jean-Drusilla. In the story's opening, Self describes Simon-Arthur's accent, a strong indicator of one's class origins, as "in the middle of middle-class accents" (127), but this median status is belied by Jean-Drusilla's pretensions to an existence higher on the social scale. Her religious fervor stands in stark contradiction to her snobbery. After Hutchinson leaves, Jean-Drusilla tells her husband that Hutchinson "is a very nice man, a very Christian man. I don't imagine for a second that simply because we receive him in this fashion that he imagines we think him quality for an instant" (149). Social propriety, she believes, must be observed, and there can be little mingling of the classes even if the Dykeses are not that far removed from Hutchinson's working-class background.

As in "Inclusion®" Dykes lives in a house called Brown House located in Oxfordshire. Although he is an artist, in "Chest" Dykes's art is restricted to painting religious icons, an expression of his devout Catholicism. His religious devotion seems genuine in "Chest," which distinguishes this parallel version of Dykes from the Simon Dykes in "Inclusion®" who claims to "despise religion as a fucking opiate" (234). When he leaves one morning to speak to his landlord, Peter-Donald Hanson, about the proximity of Hanson's hunting party to the house Dykes experiences embarrassment over his inability to afford more substantial protection against the fog than a chemical mask. Hanson and his colleagues, including the local doctor named Anthony-Anthony Bohm, on the other hand, are attired in "full scuba arrangement" (154). When Simon-Arthur succumbs fatally to the fog while strolling across a golf course at the end of the story, ultimately expiring in a bunker, Hanson remarks to Bohm—both of whom are afflicted with chronic bronchitis—that it was silly of Dykes to go out into the fog without adequate protection. Hanson tactlessly adds that at least his tenant did not die on the green, thus not interfering with their game. This insensitive comment reveals how "the times bred a certain coarseness of manner in some—just as they engendered extreme sensitivity in others" (163). Such sensitivity diminishes in this story according to each character's social position.

Self's depiction of class in his early fiction is one of his methods for indicating a primary concern: the individual's relationship to his or her surroundings. Self is a writer keenly interested in taking—and distorting—such measurements. Just as Swift exaggerated scale in *Gulliver's Travels* to satirize England's foibles, Self employs similar strategies in order to show the absurdity of certain contemporary obsessions. An archetypal example of this in Self's work, "Scale," immediately precedes "Chest" and in occupying the center position of *Grey Area* it functions as a fulcrum, leading to and from the other stories thematically and linearly.

A shorter version of the story appeared in the 1993 *Granta* issue of Young British Novelists,[14] and Self narrates passages of the story for the track "5 ml Barrel" on Bomb the Bass's recording *Clear*.[15] The story stands as a fair representation of Self's lasting concerns. Divided into six sections—consisting of a brief prologue, four chapter divisions entitled "Kettle," "Relative," "The Ascent," and "To the Bathroom," and an epigraph headed "Lizard"—the story is a first-person account written by a divorced novelist and drug addict, a man who, according to a brief allusion in "Inclusion®," is friends with a man named Gainsford, the research director at Cryborg Pharmaceuticals who recruits Zack Busner (214). The narrator's chief preoccupation, other than morphine, rests with the British roadway system, a system that provides him with a series of emotional and cognitive reference points. This is an early manifestation, in fact, of Self's own personal and narrative interest in the nexus between geography and psychic states, the so-called psycho-geography that provides a tangible shape for personal experiences. Indeed, the narrator believes that roadway signs and the layout of the motorway system can divulge historical secrets, marking him as a kind of motorway shaman.

Writers such as Iain Sinclair share Self's interest in roadways, and Sinclair's *London Orbital* concerns a peripatetic journey around the path of the M25. However, it is J. G. Ballard whose work looms large over "Scale," as it does over much of Self's early fiction. Ballard's novels *Crash* and *Concrete Island* especially seem to have an influence on Self's interest in the narrative potential of the English motorway system, and in creating from those roadways a postmodern mythology as his characters struggle to find a method of comprehending their environment and the human psyche in a technocentric world. Self's narrator in "Scale" shares with Sinclair a belief in temporal simultaneity of the motorways as a form of psychogeography. This rises to the level of lifelong obsession in "Scale," becoming less of a grand epiphanic discovery than a totalizing manic preoccupation. As Will Eaves notes in the *TLS,* "*Grey Area* describes our inability to discriminate between useful and bogus knowledge with damning ferocity."[16] However spurious the narrator's claims regarding the value of his newly devised poetic genre of "Motorway Verse" (105) and other similar mania might appear, his interest seems authentic enough. For his part Self has written of his own obsession with motorways, one he has had since childhood, claiming in "Mad about Motorways" to have become "a connoisseur of service stations, a seeker after complex gyratory systems."[17] Self draws upon personal experience in "Scale," displaying his ability to poke fun at himself just as much as he excoriates social failings in his fiction.

"Kettle," the opening section of the story, following the epigraphic prologue, introduces the narrator's addiction to morphine, which he prepares in his own kitchen, and his obsession with motorways. He plans to write a thesis entitled "No Services: Reflex Ritualism and Modern Motorway Signs (with special reference to the M40)," an endeavor for which he has neither a grant nor a commission to write, factors that fall in line with the obscurity of his subject. The "Relative" section supplies additional information about the narrator's life, such as the disparity between his residence in a bungalow, situated near a toyish-scale village located in Beaconsfield—which he disguised to appear as if it were in fact part of the model village, conning a tax assessor into believing that the narrator "was a doctoral student writing a thesis on 'The Apprehension of Scale in *Gulliver's Travels,* with special reference to Lilliput'" and that he leased the house in order to "gain first-hand experience of Gulliver's state of mind" (104)—and his ex-wife's comfortable home in the fashionable St. John's Wood section of London. He is also the author of five police procedurals featuring a Greek Cypriot detective named Inspector Archimedes and is working on a sixth entitled *Murder on the Median Strip,* a title that nominally alludes to Ballard's *Concrete Island.* Considering the manuscript of his novel-in-progress, the narrator voices a concern that equally applies to his views on the motorway system and to Self's fiction: "I begin to feel that I've painted myself into a corner with this convoluted plot. I realise that I may have tried to stretch the credulity of my potential readers too far" (103).

The story's title carries several meanings and is typical of Self's work in that each of these meanings plays some role within the work. Throughout the course of this monologue the narrator takes measurements, both of his life and of his work, as he seeks to find his niche in life. He envisages the motorway system and its arterial roads and lay-bys as a macrocosm of his own circulatory system, giving him a defined image that compensates for the emotional and physical flux in his life. Such a method of measurement is essential for him. As he notes at the beginning (and returns to at the end) of the story, he has lost not a sense of proportion but his "sense of scale" (93). Proportion for him is comparative in only the absolute while scale conveys also areas of imaginative possibility. Additionally "scale" refers to weight, such as the scales used in his preparation of morphine or the bathroom scale on which he had an adulterous assignation with his child's nanny and which, as a result, permanently registered the couple's combined weight. The narrator's father condemns his books as having "no sense of scale" (103) in the manner of Victorian fiction. Moreover, "scale" denotes texture, the "scaly hide" (103) of a lizard and the scaling of morphine granules after being baked. Finally, the word also represents linear movement, an ascent following his descents in scale that mark his psychic condition in an analogous method to "the ebb and flow of [his] opiate addiction," a fluctuation that he has "come to prize as a source of literary inspiration" (107). These multiple meanings suggest, possibly, the narrator's desire to recover his sense of scale in all its multitudes while he is supposedly demonstrating how he has retained his sense of proportion.

Grey Area is, like *The Quantity Theory of Insanity,* a well-structured collection with individual stories taking on the role of chapters in a novel. Longer and more stylistically varied than *The Quantity Theory of Insanity, Grey Area* serves partly as an elaboration on Self's fictional world and narrative techniques. Self's maturation as a writer is evident in its themes and treatment, but is perhaps most prominent in his skilled manipulation of narrative perspective. His following story collections, *Tough, Tough Toys for Tough, Tough Boys* and *Dr Mukti and Other Tales of Woe* contain several exceptional stories but lack this same degree of tight structure. The collection abounds with instances of people encountering areas of ill-defined morality or certainty, whether in the collision of academic philosophy and supernatural eroticism in "Incubus or The Impossibility of Self-Determination as to Desire,"[18] Zack Busner's ethical abnegations and criminal actions, or the physical and psychological spaces that are traversed throughout the volume.

CHAPTER SIX

London Noir
The Sweet Smell of Psychosis and
Tough, Tough Toys for Tough, Tough Boys

Although much of *My Idea of Fun* takes place in London, the novel's focus lies principally in its protagonist's mindset; in terms of the novel's topography, Sussex rather than London seems more important to the book's events. With *The Sweet Smell of Psychosis* (1996), his third novella, Self imagines a London that establishes the prototype for his subsequent longer works. Fictional locations stand in close proximity to recognizable landmarks, further deepening the duality of Self's fictional world as strange and familiar. Crucially the city also becomes a veritable ground zero of decadent proclivities that furnish the drug-laden background of his "London noir" trilogy, which consists of *The Sweet Smell of Psychosis* and the first and last stories in *Tough, Tough Toys for Tough, Tough Boys* (1998).

The term "noir" conveys several closely related meanings. Etymologically "noir" is the French term for "black," which gives rise to the literary phrase *roman noir,* or "black novel." Generally so-called noir novels contain a bleak tone and pessimistic worldview and evolve from the Gothic novels of the eighteenth and nineteenth centuries. Often sensational in terms of their sexual and violent content, they frequently feature antiheroes who become immersed in a criminal underworld. In the United States, authors such as James M. Cain, Raymond Chandler, and Dashiell Hammett developed many of the conventions associated with such works, and the cinema adaptations of their novels increased the genre's popularity. More recent practitioners include the American writer James Ellroy and the British novelist Derek Raymond. The genre's characteristic urban settings reflect its psychological darkness and moral ambiguities. Self's London noir trilogy does not feature wisecracking private investigators or stereotypical femmes fatales, but it relates to the *roman noir* in its presiding gloominess and focus on moral uncertainties. Enlightenment high ideals such as reason, free will, and individualism have surrendered to irrationality and mass conformity, and Self delivers a bleak prognosis on the human condition.

Rather than taking on the characteristics of its inhabitants, London plays a determining role in its residents' lives. Richard Hermes, the central character in *The Sweet Smell of Psychosis,* initially sees in London the alluring promises of social mobility and personal freedom but finds instead that he has become virtually incarcerated in a culture ripe with decadent hedonism and superficiality. London stands in this novella as a metaphorical prison, an anachronistic version of Jeremy Bentham's panopticon—literally, an "all-seeing" prison, constructed so that the interior remains visible from a single vantage point—with the city streets leading to and from the city's social center. The ubiquity of Bell, a "superhack" journalist and media celebrity whose image gazes out from numerous billboards and placards, reinforces his character's role as the overseer. With "The Nonce Prize," the concluding story in the trilogy, Self moves from a metaphorical prison to an actual one, the Wandsworth panopticon. Each of the trilogy's works imagines the city from the ground up, presenting a social cross-section of metropolitan indulgence; prostitutes, drug dealers, media personalities, and members of all social classes frolic in an atmosphere of murky decadence.

The Sweet Smell of Psychosis—the title alludes to Alexander Mackendrick's 1957 movie *The Sweet Smell of Success* but also points toward an important sensory component of the novella— includes several illustrations by Martin Rowson, whose drawings complement the text by rendering key scenes faithfully from the novella while also displaying the illustrator's penchant for caricature. These illustrations visually chart a Hogarthian rake's progress that also evokes Ralph Steadman's collaborations with gonzo journalist Hunter S. Thompson. Such connections are significant. In the eighteenth century the painter and engraver William Hogarth was one of England's leading satirists, and through series of works such as *The Rake's Progress* he depicted scenes of a London rife with moral dissolution. Rowson's illustrations amplify these themes in Self's text. At the center of *The Sweet Smell of Psychosis* are members of London's media establishment, but instead of acting as cultural mediators they are in fact mediated themselves by sex, drugs, alcohol, and the dubious quality of fame.

At its basic level, the premise of the story seems quite traditional, with many variations in English fiction: a young, naïve person from the provinces comes to London seeking success only to be corrupted by the trappings of metropolitan dissipation. Novels from the eighteenth century onward have juxtaposed northern England and London through a central protagonist, and Self continues in this tradition. Richard Hermes, the novella's protagonist, descends from the literary genealogy of John Boot in Evelyn Waugh's media satire, *Scoop*. After Richard publishes a few features in London magazines he exchanges his job "on the news desk of a homely, old newspaper, in a homely, old northern city"[1]—as well as his equally plain girlfriend—for an editorial position on a London magazine called *Rendezvous* and its concomitant membership among London's corps of hack journalists. These representatives of the new generation of Grub Street scribblers seek a peculiar simulacrum of celebrity status: recognition among their peers in the West End's trendy Sealink Club "that premier preening place, that atelier of arrogance" (13).

The Sealink Club is a lightly fictionalized version of London's fashionable Groucho Club, which Self has similarly called "a very atelier of arrogance, a palace of preening."[2] Emphasizing the liquidity of moving between his fictional and actual settings, Self inserts the Groucho Club into the novella where it is eclipsed by its fictional counterpart. Unlike the actual Groucho with what Self terms its "paradoxical, snobbish egalitarianism,"[3] the Sealink endorses a celebrity hierarchy, an inverse elitism based on the cultural popularity of hack journalists and media personalities. After a year in London, Richard gradually advances through the periphery of fame. He receives a promotion to Preview Editor of *Rendezvous;* one advantage of Richard's promotion is "the speedy advancement of his candidature for election to the Sealink Club" (66).[4] At the Sealink, Richard joins the group of hangers-on to Bell, whose ubiquitous presence across the print and broadcast media categorizes him as a postmodern Renaissance Man and the "grand panjandrum" (15) of the Sealink's hack clientele.

Bell has a syndicated column in two national newspapers, a weekly television chat show called *Campanology,* and a weekly radio program; one of his "most sycophantic acolytes had established . . . that there must, logically, be at least two hundred thousand people in Britain who did *nothing else* but listen to

Bell's voice, watch Bell's face, or read his words, for every waking hour of their lives" (15–16). His cultural saturation and flair for self-aggrandizement place Bell at the top of the Sealink Club's hierarchy of dubious accomplishment. The club's members include representatives from seemingly all aspects of the cultural media but the parasitic hacks signify the Sealink's principal denizens. Distinguished from "principled journalists" and "hardened reporters," these hacks and superhacks are "transmitters of trivia, broadcasters of banality, and disseminators of drek" (10) who incestuously replicate their own media to produce nothing of cultural or social relevance. This coterie of hack writers fictionalizes the writers associated not only with the broadsheet and tabloid newspapers but also with magazines like the *Modern Review,* which by billing itself as "low culture for highbrows" sought to redefine the parameters of cultural taste and literary standing. Just as Bell and his followers are inescapably associated with the Sealink Club, the *Modern Review* editors and contributors, including Self, continue to be connected in the public consciousness with the Groucho.[5]

Accordingly, a hack himself, Richard Hermes (as his name implies) serves as a herald of the gods—those who, like Bell, are the "superhacks," "the stars of his own profession" (13)—whose words and deeds Richard announces to the public. By placing Bell at the head of this group and consequently of the Sealink, Self ridicules celebrity as essentially inconsequential and laden with artificial value. Moreover, the widespread influence of these sham cultural authorities underscores the failings of a society that Self frequently depicts as enmeshed in a decadent orgy of ephemeral and superficial experiences. Richard and other characters float in a chaotic orbit around Bell, whose very hollowness creates this gravitational attraction. His is a culture of superficial importance utterly devoid of gravitas or authority.

Where Bell embodies Richard's image of professional and material success, Ursula Bentley signifies his sexual ideal. The author of a diary column called "Peccadillo" for a glossy monthly magazine, Ursula appears to Richard "not simply beautiful, but beautiful in a way that was so vastly improbable . . . that to Richard, silly fool, she redeemed him, her, all of the sordity and spoor, the tragic bathos that he felt sloshing about the Sealink" (14). Ursula exudes a powerful erotic attraction, which Richard associates with Jicki, the perfume that he considers to be her particular scent: "The odour of Jicki came off her like musk off a lioness" (83). Along with the sensitivity of his other senses, which links him to seminal Decadent synaesthetes such as Des Esseintes in Joris-Karl Huysmans's *À rebours,* Richard takes particular notice of smells. This idiosyncrasy also signals his ultimate descent into a surreal nightmare triggered by the smell of Jicki, fashioning the novella's eponymous "sweet smell of psychosis." The sexual associations that he projects on to Ursula's perfume foment his desire for Ursula and all that she represents, placing Richard in a rivalry among Bell's acolytes to replace this "grand panjandrum" as her lover. Having initially wished to conquer the media world, Richard eventually sets out to make an "assault on Mount Ursula" (78). This will, he believes, provide him with the culminating experience through which he could claim metropolitan success.

Ursula's perfume underpins in Richard's imagination an erotic duality of attraction and apparent inaccessibility, which he associates with her presumed wealth. On occasions when Richard finds her even more alluring and accessible, his sense of ease with her results from the absence of Jicki—"that scent, that sweet, ineffable, seductive perfume. . . . And with the scent gone she was more approachable, more girl-next-door than was altogether credible" (68). Richard's idealized image of Ursula exacerbates the sexual and class gulfs between her and the Soho prostitutes who ply their trade across from the Sealink Club. As Richard and Todd Reiser, another of Bell's followers, watch a prospective john enter a prostitute's room in the opening pages, Richard attempts to conjure the sights and smells of her room: "Richard imagined the odour of the place, compounded of the cheapest of perfumes, cigarette smoke, legions of cocks, more legions of condoms. Over it all the almost faecal odour of baby oil" (3). In his imagination the prostitute's bedroom conveys the same fetid atmosphere as the Sealink and London, an olfactory microcosm of unaffected decadence and its detritus, and by contrast Ursula imparts an ideal of erotic potential. This illusion is shattered at the novella's close as Richard undergoes his rite of passage into Bell's clique; as Richard finally attains his sexual goal, Ursula morphs into Bell: "the scent of Jicki came into the back of Richard's throat. But it was no longer sweet, it was bitter, bitter as cocaine" (89).

Is Richard schizophrenic, or is he caught unprepared in a society that has descended into psychosis? These are two of the novella's pivotal questions, which Self never wholly resolves. Such ambiguities constitute a major strength of Self's fiction by allowing for plausible competing interpretations, and much of his work demonstrates the inadequacies of such dichotomous viewpoints by suggesting further possibilities. While *The Sweet Smell of Psychosis* documents Richard's full initiation into the surreal dystopia of London and its mass-media carnival, it also demonstrates the very process of the "annihilation of affect" (19) that people like Bell fashion. In this respect the ability to empathize or sympathize is not only blunted but extinguished, creating a kind of terminal madness of destructive behavior. Even though Self might appear to adopt a nihilistic pose, his satiric methods stem from a sincere moral perspective—one trained not only on the superficiality of fame and the mass media, "the howling vacuity" of Bell's clique (66), but also on the pervasive influence of social class in British culture.

What martinis were to the Algonquin wits cocaine is to the denizens of the Sealink Club; Bell and his acolytes exist in a sort of perpetual culinary communion—a Burroughsian naked lunch —with the then-head of Colombia's Medellin Cartel. While one member of Bell's group has "already had dinner with Pablo . . . other cliquers had snacked with Mr Escobar" (51). Through a combination of free indirect discourse and objective critiques, Self presents the phrase as an example of, from his characters' point of view, epigrammatic wit, then exposes its inherent ephemeral and trivial quality by parenthetically stating that the Pablo Escobar shibboleth is adopted as "the clique's preferred euphemism—this month—for doing cocaine" (51). Self uses the phrase, which changes slightly in each instance, to emphasize the intrinsic remoteness between these consumers of the narcotic and its source. While Bell, Richard, and the other characters jokingly romanticize their patronage of international drug empires in an attempt to gain a sense of street credence, they remain firmly locked inside class divisions.

Self underscores the class associations between particular intoxicants and their users when Bell's group leaves the comfort of their West End haunts for London's East End. As Bell's clique —consisting in this scene of Richard, Ursula, and Mearns—travels to Limehouse their taxi driver informs them that he is an exiled Syrian air force general who had "become disgusted by the decadence" of life under the Assad regime, leading to a failed assassination attempt on President Assad (53). This scene establishes the inability of Bell and his acolytes to observe anything of significance beyond their own sybaritic pleasures; only Richard takes serious note of the cab driver's story. Alluding to a similar journey in Oscar Wilde's *The Picture of Dorian Gray,* which Self later retells in *Dorian,* Bell's gang visits a Limehouse opium den owned by an elderly Chinese immigrant. The house functions as a microcosm of multiethnic decadence, and drugs signify respective social classes and ethnicity alike: "Two Iranians sat on phallic bolsters, moodily chasing the dragon; on a velveteen-covered divan a gaggle of giggling upper-class girls—as out of their element as gorillas in Regent's Park—were high on E, stroking each other's hair; and as the clique climbed the stairs, they passed two black guys smoking crack in a pipe made from a Volvic bottle" (58). The Limehouse passage also illustrates the frequent nesting of Self's fiction as characters who are the protagonists of certain works have cameos in others, strengthening the cohesion of his *roman-fleuve,* a series of closely allied works that features recurring characters. In the opium-den episode, Self briefly introduces Danny O'Toole, one of the men smoking crack from a Volvic bottle, who then becomes the focus of the opening and closing stories of *Tough, Tough Toys for Tough, Tough Boys* that complete his London noir trilogy.[6]

Depicting the bleak consequences of the hedonistic metropolitan attitude so predominant at the end of the twentieth century, Self's London noir sequence presents this period as a decadent extension of the gratuitous consumption from the 1980s. That decade imparted other social legacies, creating what Self views as a significant cultural change. In his perceptive essay on English culture, "The Valley of the Corn Dollies," Self contends that during "the eighties we saw rickets and tuberculosis reappear in our cities; along with new kids on the block: firearms and crack cocaine, and I would argue that as a direct result England came of age as a particular kind of culture."[7] Where Richard Hermes, Bell, and Ursula Bentley inhabit a society of cocaine-enhanced illusions and middle-class pleasures, Danny comes from the "new crack city"[8] of violence and crack cocaine. "The London street drug scene is as subject to the caste principle as any other part of London," Self has written; "druggies identify one another by eye contact and little else."[9] Through Danny and his background Self focuses on the working-class aspects of the drug culture, juxtaposing them against the privileged, white middle-class segment of society that he depicts as viewing drugs as simply another commodity for their convenient consumption.

"The Rock of Crack as Big as the Ritz," the first story in *Tough, Tough Toys for Tough, Tough Boys,* provides the expository details of Danny O'Toole's ill-fated entry into dealing drugs with his younger brother, Tembe. Born as Bantu, Danny rejects the name and its patina of African identity. "Our mother thought they was cool and African," he tells his brother of their birth names, "but she knew nothing, man, bugger all. The Bantu were a fucking *tribe,* man, and as for Tembe, thass jus' a style of fucking *music.*"[10] He leaves London for Jamaica, where in Kingston he begins working for a drug dealer called Skank, and adopts the moniker "London." After a year under Skank's tutelage, he begins to exhaust his opportunities in the violent Jamaican drug trade: "A year muscling rock in Trenchtown was about as full an apprenticeship as anyone could serve. This was a business where you moved straight from work experience to retirement, with not much of a career in between" (5). Due to his loyalty and capability—and his unflagging policy of personal abstention from crack—"London" is sent to Philadelphia to head a crew of Jamaican drug dealers. Just as the shallow hedonism of 1990s London in *The Sweet Smell of Psychosis* reflects an extension of the decadent 1980s, in "The Rock of Crack as Big as the Ritz" Self draws an analogy between the drug trade and capitalism. Operating in "the back end of a decade that was big on enterprise" (5), "London" demonstrates his entrepreneurial skill. Drug dealing "was like running any retail concern anywhere: stock control, margins, managerial problems" (6), and he steals three kilos from Skank and returns to England. Back in London, he drops his adopted name and—once again with his destiny reflecting broader social fortunes—he remains jobless and nameless in the economic recession of 1991. He joins the army for a two-year tour during the Gulf War and begins calling himself "Danny." Following his stint in the army, Danny returns to his northwest London suburb of Harlesden and the house he purchased with the proceeds from double-crossing Skank. The army experience changes Danny from a "fucked-up, angry, potentially violent, coloured youth" to a leaner, "frustrated, efficient, angry black man" (7). Additionally his combat experience in Iraq caused guns and violence no longer to hold any attraction for him, and Danny vows to avoid falling back into drug dealing. While renovating his house, Danny begins tearing down a cellar wall and discovers a large, inexplicable seam of crack cocaine.

As he attempts to assess the size of this improbable crack vein by measuring it with plumbing rods, Danny concludes "that the entire house must be underpinned by an enormous rock of crack" (10), one "big enough to flood the market for crack in London, perhaps even the whole of Europe" (11). The story produces its own internal logic, and like Kafka, Gogol, and writers in the magical realist tradition, Self does not attempt to explain the genesis of this absurd conceit. Both the story's title and this titular image are an obvious and fitting homage to F. Scott Fitzgerald's 1922 short story "The Diamond as Big as the Ritz."[11]

Fitzgerald's short-fiction masterpiece satirizes extreme wealth and the corresponding delusion that material possessions represent virtue by depicting the inhumane self-interest and greed that accompanies Braddock Washington's legacy of inheriting a mountain comprising an enormous diamond. Danny O'Toole and Fitzgerald's protagonist, John T. Unger, could not seem further apart: Danny is a poorly educated, working-class black Englishman who lives on the social margins, trying to avoid attention from the police and drug syndicates alike; Unger is a sixteen-year-old white American who hails from a prominent family and attends the world's most exclusive prep school. Both characters, however, become ensnared to different extents by their attachments to the wealthy and the corruptive influence of greed. Self points out that drug addiction is essentially a form of avarice, feeding an insatiable lust.

Danny exploits this as he resumes his career in the crack trade, taking care not to sample his product or to carry it on his person. With Tembe as his runner, Danny sells first to the local Afro-Caribbean population and then begins cultivating a clientele of wealthy white addicts in the City and West End, finding himself "in the darkest and tackiest regions of decadence" (12). Within a few months Danny's clientele includes "a clique of true high-lowlife" in a wealthy Iranian named Masud, who has taken up residence in Piccadilly at the Ritz, and his accompanying "gaggle of rich kids whose inverse ratio of money-to-sense was simply staggering" (13). With Masud as his primary customer, Danny augments his crack trade with heroin, expanding his market. As Tembe makes multiple daily deliveries to Masud's suite at the Ritz he falls deeper into addiction himself, discovering that the "whole hit of rock is to want *more rock*. The buzz of rock is itself the wanting of *more rock*" (21).

Although Self is often accused of glamorizing their use, he consistently presents drugs in negative terms. However playful the title of "The Rock of Crack as Big as the Ritz" might seem, the story imparts at least two serious warnings concerning drugs: that addiction can come rapidly and with devastating consequences, psychologically and financially; and that drug trafficking is a dangerous business, one that too many members of the social underclass view as their only available option. While the cognoscenti in *The Sweet Smell of Psychosis* perceive drugs as a recreational liberty and indulgence, the O'Toole brothers regard drugs as central to their life. Perhaps the greatest attribute of "The Rock of Crack as Big as the Ritz" lies in its treatment of the working-class drug trade. As fantastic as the main conceit of the inexplicable crack source is, the story retains a gritty overtone.

A chief part of the story's tension lies in the pervasive threat of retribution from Skank and the Yardies—the nickname for Jamaican drug dealers. While this never materializes and Danny grows increasingly bold in his drug trade, he also risks gaining attention from competing dealers, a fact of which he is fully aware: "And those Yardies had no respect. They were like monkeys just down from the fucking trees—so Danny admonished Tembe—they didn't care about any law, white or black, criminal or straight" (11). This passage comes nearly verbatim from "New Crack City," an earlier article in which Self examines the London crack trade, noting that like the white dealers the English black dealers are equally "dismissive" of the Jamaican gangs. In this article a black drug dealer named Bruno remarks, "Yardies? They're just down from the trees, man." [12] By fictionalizing it from Danny's perspective, Self invests his story with heightened verisimilitude as well as suggesting Danny's own racial prejudice. That Danny persists in dealing crack and heroin despite being fully cognizant of the inherent dangers in the drug culture suggests a degree of hubris on his part, one stemming from the allure of wealth he associates with dealing.

"The Nonce Prize" continues Danny's story, picking it up three years later in 1996. Five years have elapsed since Danny stole three kilos of Skank's product in Philadelphia, and his subsequent careless behavior in London has come to his former employer's attention. As the story opens, Danny and Tembe have exchanged roles: the younger brother now gives orders, and Danny has developed a sixty-pipe-a-day crack habit. Worse still, his supply of crack has disappeared: "after a couple of years of very high living the seam was gone, and at around the same time Danny, feeling wrung out by the experience, had taken his first pipe of crack and discovered what he always sus-pected; that, in this most unnatural of pursuits, he turned out to be a natural" (181). He is now "no longer the master puppeteer —merely a puppet on a pipe" (182).

Self quickly shows how far Danny has fallen and how he is set up for Skank to take revenge. Traveling under the assumed name of Joseph Andrews, Skank arrives in London to arrange Danny's murder.[13] Skank learns of Danny's presence in London through a Chinese immigrant whose house in Limehouse Danny frequents. As Self revisits the Limehouse scene from *The Sweet Smell of Psychosis* from Danny's point of view, what previously appeared as insignificant acquires magnitude. This demonstrates the expanded dimension of Self's fictional world while further suggesting the encompassing self-absorption of Bell and his fol-lowers who, with the exception of Mearns's flippant remark to Danny, barely register their presence. Now Bell and his clique are reduced to anonymity. As Danny trains his attention on smoking crack from a Volvic bottle, his companion, Bruno, observes Bell and his followers and has "pegged them as West End media types, out for a night's drug slumming" (191). As Mearns makes a sarcastic comment, Danny replies "Whassit t'you, cunt!" (191). The shift in punctuation—Danny's reply is an interrogative in *The Sweet Smell of Psychosis*—underscores this change in perspective. Thus what for Bell's clique is a night of "drug slumming" is effectively for Danny the end of his former life.

"The Nonce Prize" contains an even more noticeable tonal shift from the cool satire of *The Sweet Smell of Psychosis* and "Rock of Crack" to one of genuine pathos. Danny's story is a modern tragedy, a fact that Self emphasizes by having Danny imagine seeing the Fates bearing down on him. Although he is not killed, he is beaten, abducted, and subsequently framed for the rape and murder of a six-year-old boy. The actual assailants, an enforcer transplanted from Bournemouth to London's "stygian underworld" (195) named Gerald and his accomplice, Shaun Withers, met during a treatment program for sexual offenders while at prison. United in their desire to act upon a mutual fantasy—"the abduction, buggering, torture, mutilation and eventual murder of a young boy, the younger the better" (194)—they lure their victim from a Stoke Newington playground, then rape him for ten days before killing him. Self's fiction from this period forward contains notable episodes of children's tragic fates—possibly a result of his natural anxieties as a father—and they achieve poignancy not just from the brutal violation of a child's innocence but from a concomitant abuse of trust.

Gary, the six-year-old victim, goes willingly to Gerald's car, perhaps owing to his history as a victim of domestic abuse. After Danny awakes to find himself in bed with Gary's mutilated body, the scene moves from an account of the sadistic horror of the boy's murder to culminate in a seemingly mundane detail that suddenly gains a dreadful pathos, which Self accentuates by showing the progression of Danny's startled consciousness. Beginning with concise, journalistic descriptions the scene culminates in a final sentence of suspended cadences and paratactic subordination: "Danny registered blond hair, pulped features, cut throat. There was a lot of blood. The child's hands and feet had been severed and left beside the corpse, which was naked from the waist down. The last thing Danny took in before he began, simultaneously, to puke and scream, was that the little boy was wearing a bright sweatshirt, featuring a decal of the character Buzz Lightyear from the movie *Toy Story*" (194). The boy's rape and murder are horrific enough in fiction, but throughout "The Nonce Prize" Self's fictional world seems indistinct from actuality; the 1993 murder of James Bulger, a two-year-old Liverpool boy killed by a pair of ten-year-olds, and accounts of vanished and murdered children in Andrew O'Hagan's *The Missing* (1995) provide real-life analogues for Self's fictional account.

Danny, too, is a victim. Framed for the boy's rape and murder—Danny's semen had been injected into Gary's mouth and anus, recalling the icing gun scene of "Cock"—he is sentenced to life in prison with a minimum recommendation of twenty years. As a convicted sexual offender, a "nonce," the sentence practically ensures his violent death in prison: "Danny had been around enough to hear the stories about what happened to sex offenders inside. He knew about juggings and shavings and socks full of pool balls. He had heard tell of how the 'normal' offenders plotted to get their hands on nonces; how even a fairly low crim'—a crack-head, a larcenist, whatever—could vastly improve his status by doing a nonce. Behind those high walls slathered with anti-climb paint there was only ever one season; an open one for nonces" (201–2). Danny is placed in F Wing of HMP Wandsworth, a panopticon prison. On F Wing pedophiles are protected by being isolated from the prison's general population. In an effort to maintain his self-respect Danny wants to be reassigned to A Wing. Having been told by the prison's warden that he should "do something useful" in prison (216), Danny enrolls in a creative writing course under the impression that it was a vocational course—"Creative Wiring" (220)—and that he would learn a trade.

The students in the creative writing course—Danny and two other convicted sex offenders, Philip Greenslade and Sidney Cracknell—"exemplify the three commonest types of wannabee writer" (225). Greenslade, who had abducted, tortured, raped, and murdered an eleven-year-old girl, fits into the mold of the "relentless, prosaic plodder" (225), and litters his prose with banal clichés. Greenslade's writing becomes an extension of his psychopathology: "The only thing to indicate that this story was written by a man with an unconscious as dark as a black hole was the peculiar absence of affect. The author might have felt for his creations in the abstract, but on the page he manipulated them like wooden puppets, like victims" (225). Cracknell, who embodies the "compulsive scribbler" (225), had been writing a futuristic science fiction saga consisting of some five million handwritten words. Initially, the course instructor, Gerry Mahoney, identifies Danny as the third stereotype: "the writer who can't write" (228). Danny dedicates himself to completing an informal adult literacy course, dutifully completing the grammatical exercises that Mahoney gives him and proceeding "to read his way through every single book available in the meager nonce-wing library" (229).

As Danny progresses through the course, eventually discovering his talent for writing, he and the others enter a creative writing competition for prison inmates, the Wolfenden Prize for Prison Writing. An ironic allusion to the 1957 Report of the Wolfenden Committee, which argued for the legalization of homosexual behavior between consenting adults and helped pave the way for decriminalization under the Sexual Offences Act a decade later, the Wolfenden Prize semantically becomes the "nonce" prize. Although Self has been involved with awards similar to the fictional Wolfenden Prize—judging the 2003 Andrew Groves Short Story Competition and in the same year opening the annual Koestler Exhibition of prisoner art—Danny's discovery of his talent for writing appears to be inspired by Self's friendship with Noel "Razors" Smith, a convicted armed robber and author of the memoir *A Few Kind Words and a Loaded Gun* (2004), a book that Self helped get published.

The three inmates enact a smallscale literary culture, complete with rivalry, as they vie for the relative distinction and fame that the award confers, along with petty jealousies and accusations of intellectual theft. Self constructs an extended metaphor of writing as a form of incarceration in that both carry an imposed isolation and focus myopically at times on their respective sentences. In doing so, Self deflates the pretensions that writers and readers might affect and idealistically attribute to writing. This becomes patently clear after the indolent novelist Cal Devenish places Danny, Greenslade, and Cracknell on his shortlist for the Wolfenden Prize. Devenish speculates that Cracknell's meaningless compacted prose "might be a satire on the ephemerality of contemporary culture; narrative itself characterised as a non-biodegradable piece of packaging, littering the verge of the cosmos" (238) and that Greenslade's entry is similarly ironic, "one of the cleverest and most subtle portrayals of the affectless, psychopathic mind that he had ever read" (238) and an example of a "compelling moral ironist" (243).

Danny's story—essentially, "The Rock of Crack as Big as the Ritz"—contains "magical realist elements that never quite jibed" and Devenish "could never decide whether to come down on the side of phonetic transcription of non-standard English, or not" (238). The award becomes another form of injustice. Aptly for a budding writer, Danny is the victim of misreading. The judicial system had wrongly regarded him as a sex offender and murderer, and Devenish misjudges Danny's writing just as he does the other finalists' work and their physical appearance. Devenish realizes his error only when he names Greenslade the winner and realizes that Greenslade's writing contains no ironic distance, that he actually is a psychopath (243). In addition to the prize and the attention it could bestow on its recipient, Greenslade also receives another reward Danny strives for: transfer from the nonce wing.

The six stories in *Tough, Tough Toys for Tough, Tough Boys* that separate "The Rock of Crack as Big as the Ritz" and "The Nonce Prize" are less thematically linked than many of the stories in Self's previous collections. "Flytopia" is set in the Suffolk town of Inwardleigh and shows the symbiotic relationship that develops between an index compiler named Jonathan Priestley and the insects that inhabit his cottage on Hogg Lane, alluding to James Hogg—as does the reference in "The Quantity Theory of Insanity" to Euan MacLintock's housekeeper, Mrs. Hogg, who is "wedded to Calvinist fatalism."[14] In "A Story for Europe," Self has a two-year-old English boy, Humphrey Green, and a sixty-one-year-old German banker, Martin Zweijärig ("two-year-old") exchange speech patterns; "Humpy" speaks fluent business German while Zweijärig suddenly exhibits increasingly childish behavior and outbursts, which are attributed to the onset of a stroke. "Caring, Sharing," the fifth story in the volume, is set in a futuristic Manhattan where people keep "emotos," large, genetic mutants with the mental capabilities of children, as companions for cuddling and comfort, allowing adults to behave as children; notably, two emotos are named Dave and Jane, and a version of the emotos appears in *The Book of Dave* (2006). Of particular interest to Self's ongoing body of work, from "Understanding the Ur-Bororo" to *The Book of Dave*, "Dave Too" is a first-person account of a world inundated by men named Dave—a nominal curiosity that spreads like a virus and extends to the naming of at least one neighboring town, Davyhulme, a possible pun on the name of the eighteenth-century philosopher David Hume. The narrator's best friend, casual acquaintances in a café, strangers, and his therapist all share the name; even the narrator's former lover has applied to change her name by deed poll from Velma to Davina.

Dave Klagfarten, the psychiatrist, speculates that because "the biblical David was the individual who most completely realised the theocratic ideal of the Israelites, and that the yearning for his return became a matter of almost messianic fervour . . . it doesn't seem to stretch the analogy that far to suggest that this new pattern of emergent Daves represents something similar, a secular ultramontanism, perhaps" (81). The narrator's anonymity is a manifestation of what Klagfarten describes as the narrator's "particular brand of alienation, of depersonalisation" (81), a condition that Klagfarten treats through therapy and the antidepressant Parstelin. In effect the narrator has been excluded from much of society, enjoying neither the security of a comprehensible if homogeneous identity nor certain aspects of social intercourse. The narrator attempts to ameliorate this deracination by adopting daily routines that help to stave off lone-liness, yet lacking "Daveness," "Davidity," or "Davitude" (75) in a Dave-dominated society he cannot achieve any self-understand-ing. As a result, the narrator becomes an addict of sorts to the reg-ularity of Daves but lashes out homicidally to reduce their number by one.

Psychiatrists' effectiveness and problems involving self-awareness comprise two enduring motifs in Self's fiction, and Self takes up both themes in the linked stories concerning Bill Bywater. The works appear consecutively in *Tough, Tough Toys for Tough, Tough Boys* but in reverse chronological order. In the title story Bill Bywater has resigned as a practicing psychoana-lyst, unable to "see the virtue" in his profession, and hires him-self as a freelance intermediary to police departments and other agencies (116). His "peculiar affinity for talking down the real crazies" stems from his ability to "fully empathise with these extruded psyches, whose points of view were so vertiginous" (116). Bill, however, has his own affective difficulties; after pick-ing up a hitchhiker named Mark on the drive from the Orkneys to London, he offers various forms of assistance as a means of humiliating the man. As they drive to Glasgow, Bill elicits key bits of information from Mark after plying him with Scotch and marijuana. One of Bill's favorite games, he learns as much pos-sible about a stranger without making any personal revelations himself. Mark's name indicates his role in Bill's game as a target (133). Bill learns that Mark married young, has two children he seldom sees, and that on his way to visit them in Poole he intends to see a friend in Glasgow in order to race Tonka toys down a street—the story's title refers to a 1960s Tonka advertising slogan, and this takes an ironic aspect by referring to ideas of masculinity in adult males. Games and toys are Bill's pastimes, taking a human toll. Bill has not seen his own son in three years, and his recent life has been one of repeated breaks with lovers and others close to him.

A variation on the road narrative, "Tough, Tough Toys for Tough, Tough Boys" lacks the sense of freedom normally attached to works such as Jack Kerouac's *On the Road*. Instead, it is a suicide journey as Bill leaves the comfort and solace of Scotland to return to London. He numbs his consciousness with alcohol and marijuana, keeping a bottle of single malt Scotch hidden beneath old psychiatric journals behind his car seat. Like Bill Bywater, Dr. Anthony Bohm has also fled England for Scotland following the aftermath of the events depicted in "Inclusion®" from *Grey Area*. Self has written about the Orkneys in his journalism, and it is notable that he left England for Scotland during the media debacle following his infamous firing from the *Observer* in 1997. Through Bill Bywater's tragic road trip, Self confronts the consequences of his addictions, much as he does through the character of Natasha in *How the Dead Live* (2000). Self has said that he finds the story too poignant, telling Lynn Barber that "I realise now it's very much an anticipatory suicide note, written when I was struggling against alcoholism and really going under."[15] Bill examines his life, noting the neglect, resentment, indulgence, and cynicism that have replaced his compassion for others (153), and in a desperate bid to find something salvageable he "shuffle[s] his pack of shiny memories" (153) before steering the car off the road, presumably to his death.

The companion story, "Design Faults in the Volvo 760 Turbo," is set some three years earlier. Adopting a narrative tone and arrangement of an owner's manual that stands in heavy contrast to "Tough, Tough Toys," the story details Bill's adulterous lifestyle. Distortions of scale emerge in Self's fiction as a means of pitting an individual's psychological state against the external environment, frequently creating bizarre and ludic tensions, and in "Design Faults" Bill Bywater imagines himself in Brobdingnagian proportions as he begins an extramarital affair. In this "terrifyingly tiny world of the urban adulterer" (155), Bill sees himself as a giant, a "Colossus of Roads" (157) standing astride two lanes of traffic, making his infidelity glaringly obvious to his wife, Vanessa. Bill becomes fixated on imagining the genitalia of Serena, his new lover, and the owner's manual to his Volvo becomes charged with sexual innuendo. In an effort to separate thoughts of Serena's vulva from the make of his car, Bill first white-outs all references to the manufacturer in the manual and then removes all identifications on the automobile itself. Whereas in *My Idea of Fun* marketers strive to render popular brands as generics by status of popularity, Bill attempts to detach himself from the sexual connotations that the car suggests. Self plays with the Freudian idea of a car as metaphorical genitalia by having Bill detect sexual connotations in the manual's innocuous headings such as "Special Rims" (170). That the car's model year is the same as that of his and Vanessa's marriage exacerbates his projections of guilt onto the car. Conversely, Bill's mechanic, Dave Adler, who has been servicing the Volvo since Bill resigned his psychiatric practice years previously, views automobiles in strictly utilitarian terms. At the close of story it transpires that Adler—who hangs a sign with a Freudian allusion on his closed shop—is likewise "giving Vanessa Bywater's chassis a really thorough servicing" (174).

Although the story is laden with such puns, running the risk of devolving into verbal irony for its own sake, they demonstrate the mindset of Bill Bywater as a habitual philanderer. There is a jauntiness to the narrative technique and to Bill's pangs of guilt and conscience that lend further poignancy to "Tough, Tough Toys for Tough, Tough Boys." By reversing the chronological order of these two stories in the book, Self in effect resurrects Bill Bywater to make actual his memories in "Tough, Tough Toys," most especially the passage where Bill and Serena consummate their affair in a copse on Hampstead Heath and Bill becomes that stereotypical fictional character, the Hampstead adulterer.

The London that Bill inhabits appears remarkably distinct from that of Danny O'Toole, but both men find themselves marked as types: Bill as a bourgeois philanderer, Danny as a crackhead and nonce. Underneath these socially prescribed roles lies a more accurate reality, which both men seek to discover. All of the stories in *Tough, Tough Toys for Tough, Tough Boys* deal in one fashion or another with depictions of masculinity or adults who behave in childlike ways, demonstrating the fragile psyches of the inhabitants of Self's fictional world.

CHAPTER SEVEN

Souls in Conflict
Great Apes and *How the Dead Live*

"So I was smacked out on the Prime Minister's jet, big deal."[1]
Will Self's casual admission after initially denying that he snorted
heroin on John Major's campaign jet in April 1997 is less flippant than it might first seem. Self attempts to place the imbroglio
and the media coverage that followed it into perspective; his
remark attempts to deflect the well-documented controversy by
pointing out his actions' cultural insignificance. Nevertheless his
personal troubles became topics offered for public censure as he
wrestled once again with his addictions. In the wake of this whirl
of unbidden media coverage, he published his second novel, a
more significant event in his career.

The fourth-century Christian Latin poet Prudentius represented the conflict between virtue and vice as a battle for the soul
in his poem "Psychomachia," initiating the psychomachy genre.
While the genre includes works such as *Everyman* and Chris-
topher Marlowe's *Doctor Faustus*, "psychomachia" has since
become a general literary term for any similar contest for possession of one's soul. A unifying theme of Will Self's novels beginning with *My Idea of Fun*, this conflict corresponds also to details
in his life and helps to explain the underlying seriousness of his
depictions of drug use, addiction, and their bleak consequences.

Like Self's response to the campaign debacle, perspective lies
at the heart of *Great Apes*. As the novel opens, Simon Dykes,
an artist whose works scrutinize the human body through an

apocalyptic series of human catastrophes, including Ebola outbreaks and the 1987 fire at the King's Cross underground station, poses a question about the effects of losing your sense of perspective rather than the more universal loss of proportion. "Disastrous for a painter," his gallery agent replies.[2] Two consistent threads in Self's fiction, perspective and proportion consider respectively the way individuals view their environment and their position in it. Both concepts apply to psychological as well as physical contexts. In a 1995 article sympathetic to King Kong as a character, Self views the giant gorilla in these terms. According to Self, the image of Kong astride the Empire State Building in the 1933 film carries a mythopoeic significance: "the scene is a *Götterdämmerung,* in which a godlike figure protests against the hideous alienation of the urban scape in the most potent way imaginable."[3] Through multiple ironic and satiric inversions in *Great Apes,* Self challenges his readers to reconsider their own sense of human perspective.

Great Apes signifies an important stage in Self's maturation as a novelist. More ambitious in scope and theme than any of his previous works, the novel displays his ability to synthesize an extended metaphor along with elements of his previous fiction into a cohesive whole. Reuniting Simon Dykes and Zack Busner, now transformed into chimpanzees, *Great Apes* continues the events Self depicts in "Inclusion®" and draws upon the consequences of that story's surreptitious drug trial while also posing larger questions regarding humanism and animal rights. These ideas center on an underlying premise: that anthropocentrism—placing human beings at the center of the universe—proceeds from naïve and arrogant assumptions about humans' supremacy over all life forms and has instilled in our collective consciousness a false belief that we are uniquely conscious animals. Self examines the essential argument that the British philosopher John Gray likewise makes in *Straw Dogs* (2002).

For Gray science and religion both contain ideological dogmas that distort our perception of the world and our position in it. The "supreme value" of science, Gray writes, "may be in showing that the world humans are programmed to perceive is a chimera."[4] That is, the belief that *Homo sapiens* is a unique species in control of its destiny is a flawed conception, an illusion that has been instilled through an evolving process of philosophical, metaphysical, and theological thought. "Our image of ourselves," Gray argues, "is formed from our ingrained belief that *consciousness, selfhood,* and *free will* are what define us as human beings, and raise us above all other creatures."[5] In *Great Apes,* Self presages these main points, using the satiric trope of an inverted parallel world to expose anthropocentrism as a failed system of beliefs and to remind his readers that humans are in essence animals, not necessarily any more rational than those species most closely related to them. As Self argues in his King Kong article, the fate of apes carries potential consequences for humanity: "the destruction of our closest relatives will diminish what it is to be human—and possibly even destroy it. For without their existence to shore up our differences, will we not perhaps collapse back into the slough of bestiality we have pulled ourselves out of?"[6]

Satirists have for centuries made effective use of placing humans and other primates in inverted roles, and throughout *Great Apes,* Self refers to these and other fictional depictions. Swift's Yahoos, Thomas Love Peacock's Sir Oran Haut-Ton from *Melincourt,* Kafka's "Report to an Academy," the *Planet of the Apes* film series, and other key works permeate the novel implicitly and explicitly as a way of pointing out that doubt regarding humans' privileged position in the animal hierarchy has presented provocative images that have been equally unsettling and comic. Self establishes his species reversal through the voice of his implied author, a chimpanzee version of himself. In the author's note that prefaces the novel Self draws attention to the fictional portrayals of humans and the supposedly lower primates. "Many writers have seen in the human a paradigm for the gentler as well as the darker side of chimpanzee nature. From *Melincourt* to *My Human Wife,* from *King Kong* to the *Planet of the Humans* films, writers have flirted with the numinous dividing line between man and chimp" (x–xi). This division becomes all the more mysterious when transgressed so easily.

As with each of Self's major works, *Great Apes* contains specific connections to his previous fiction. No simple continuation of the relationship between Busner and Dykes set forth in "Inclusion®," the novel creates an additional alternative universe for the parallel world that Self's fiction typically presents. In the process these fictive worlds collide, throwing into confusion the reader's purchase on scale and perspective. Zack Busner, Simon and Jean Dykes, Anthony Bohm, Jane Bowen, Tony Valuam, and other characters carry forward their respective histories and idiosyncrasies, and Self also returns to familiar settings, most prominently Charing Cross Hospital, Grindley's restaurant, and the Sealink Club. But there have been slight adjustments: architectural scale conforms to the height of bipedal chimps rather than humans; while Julius the barman remains a constant presence at the Sealink, gone are Bell and his hack coterie from *The Sweet Smell of Psychosis,* their eminence supplanted by artists, gallery agents, and writers. The continuity between the actual world and Self's fictional worlds becomes distorted through his narrative conceit, throwing into doubt the very question of Simon's species.

Simon Dykes, the novel's principal protagonist, is identified as human in the author's note—a riposte to Self's critics who claim that he treats his characters with a lack of sympathy and "diabolic disregard" (xi)—and through the first six chapters he appears as human until he suffers a psychological breakdown, perhaps stemming from narcotic intoxication, in which his humanity is exposed as a delusion. The very scale of Simon's human delusion is unprecedented in this chimp world. In a continuation of the death-of-affect motif that characterizes much of Self's fiction, Zack Busner observes that Simon's behavior is essentially "lacking in affect," resulting in his speculation that Simon's "human delusion . . . might only have been the flamboyant onset of a condition, the chronic stage of which would be characterised by apathy, withdrawal and eventually complete mental collapse" (190). Further complicating any psychiatric understanding of this complex delusion, scans of Simon's brain reveal that some unknown trauma or generative defect has altered his simian physiology; his brain resembles that of a human (201). However, there are hints leading up to his breakdown that his chimp nature or "chimpunity" attempts to assert itself, frequently drawing attention to the scatological aspect of Self's satiric method. A memory from childhood of parental calls to return home while playing remind him of "hooting apes in the suburban gloaming" (12); standing in Oxford Circus he imagines the area "dumped upon by a giant ape," a "post-imperial Kong" and "pantagruelian pongid" (26); at the Sealink he notes that his cheek stubble has "softened to fur" (42), and he refers to his lover, Sarah Peasenhulme, as his "little monkey" (43) and comments on her "little paw" (55). Such references skillfully set the scene for Simon's apparent species-crossing following an evening of chemical and carnal ecstasy.

The resulting transformation of Simon's world, or the world as he thought he knew it, into one where chimpanzees are the dominant species because of unparalleled evolutionary success, upsets his conception of the world itself. In this world-turned-upside-down, Self upends social customs and rituals, language, morality, and other guiding principles. Monogamous sexual relationships receive public scorn in the chimp world, and younger chimps are encouraged to mate early and frequently; females are particularly sexually attractive when in oestrus, wearing swelling protectors that help to advertise this fact. Mating itself is typically a perfunctory act, accompanied by a cacophony of clacking teeth and howls. As in the human world, parental neglect entails a particularly odious form of child abuse, but in *Great Apes* fathers who fail either to mate with their daughters or to mate with them often enough become social outcasts. Many reviewers commented on this aspect of the novel's satire, and the critic for London's *Independent* observes that the chimps in *Great Apes* are not the ostensibly cute creatures from circuses, tea advertisements, and other popular images that present chimpanzees in human clothing and situations—images that Self ridicules throughout the novel. Instead, they "fight, groom, mate incessantly and at random, eat shit and live in large, fluid family groupings. When Dykes wakes up to find a giant, furry beast in his bed, we are frightened with him. Later, that same young female chimp reveals to her psychoanalyst that she was abused as a child. The reader realises slowly, and with revulsion, that in the chimp world this means that she was not mated by her alpha (or father) on a regular enough basis. It is a nasty moment, that pulls us back from the personified chimps and leaves us between worlds."[7] Tactile experiences are important to these chimpanzees, and as with mating practices mutual grooming provides a foundation for a healthy society. Chimps greet one another by pant-hooting and offering their anuses or ischial scrags for kissing before proceeding to pick dried mucus, semen, and other debris from each other's fur. As one reviewer of the novel succinctly points out, Self's "new civilisation is, needless to say, a forest of comic inversions, a world where 'you can kiss my arse' is a formal greeting, and where children are considered 'abused' if they are sexually neglected by their groups' dominant male, or 'alpha.'"[8]

Chimpanzee communication occurs primarily through non-verbal gestures, presenting Self with a narrative difficulty. For a writer so attuned to the nuances of language, including verbal puns and other implied meanings, depicting a society that uses spoken language frequently as a means of verbal emphasis poses the hazard of undermining the verisimilitude on which the novel relies in part. Self carefully sets up the dominance of sign language, including the presence of regional and class-based accents which reveal themselves through subtle alterations in hand movement, by describing such gestures and presenting tele-screens through which chimps can see each other. As a result, the narrative descriptions and dialogue are for the most part verbal translations or iterations of sign language. To demonstrate further the differences between human and simian communication, Self invents a string of neologisms that function as chimp counterparts to human language. The chimps punctuate their speech with verbal emphases, most frequently with cries of "euch-euch," "hoo," "huu," "chup-chupp," and other interjections that serve exclamatory and interrogative purposes. One point that these puns serve is to deconstruct contemporary verbal usage in such a way that it draws the reader's attention to even the most seemingly commonplace forms of expression, as

Self does also in *The Book of Dave* (2006). While these linguistic shifts can be highly entertaining they also allow for moments of seriousness as in the problem of "CIV," making readers confront not only HIV and AIDS—which in the novel may have originated from exposure to wild humans in Africa—but also the tests conducted on chimpanzees in the ongoing search for cures and other treatments.

In fact the illegal experiments that Busner conducts on Simon Dykes in "Inclusion®" form a neat complement to animal testing. Most likely consequences of the Cryborg Pharmaceuticals testing, Simon's delusional state and the physiological change to his brain structure reveal the disastrous consequences of such illicit practices. Zack Busner remains unconvinced of his role in generating his patient's psychological condition, inhabiting a psychic area "between conscious conscience and guilty unconsciousness" (82), but he accepts responsibility to help Simon to reconnect with his essential chimpunity. Busner also is prepared to accept full responsibility when a medical ethics board begins to investigate charges against him. Anthony Bohm, the Oxfordshire general practitioner, appears more willing to admit his complicity privately, and his guilty conscience suggests one reason why Bohm has relocated to the remote Scottish island of Papa Westray in "Tough, Tough Toys for Tough, Tough Boys." In one of the novel's plot lines, David Gambol, Busner's research assistant, Kevin Whatley, the head of the psychiatric staff at Charing Cross Hospital, and Phillips, a former Cryborg researcher now dying of AIDS, conspire to topple Busner from his dubious position in the social and psychiatric hierarchies. Phillips possesses evidence of Busner's involvement in the Inclusion testing: a folder of data and reports that could be the same files that comprise the narrative of "Inclusion®" itself. This cabal releases their evidence to the General Medical Council, which investigates Busner and suspends his medical license. Although a significant plot line in its own right, most especially for depicting the ephemeral position at the head of a simian social pecking order, it reveals the degrees to which Busner's and Dykes's fate have become conjoined, lending an ironic meaning to Busner's claims in "Inclusion®" that he has "been included within the psyche of Simon Dykes in a most perverse fashion."[9]

The relationship between Busner and Dykes gets at the center of the artist's aesthetic intentions, with the self-proclaimed "anti-psychiatrist" serving intermittently as an interpreter of Dykes's work. Moreover, Busner notes the synchronous nature between his professional aims and Dykes's artistic objectives. Simon's paintings record disastrous events such as passengers trapped on an escalator at the King's Cross underground station as a fire rages; the fuselage of a Boeing 747 ripping apart after a bomb detonates in a painting called *Aerial Chartres;* and, in one entitled *Flat Pack Stops at Ebola,* shoppers at an Ikea store bleeding out fatally after contracting Ebola. Each of these paintings situates a helpless infant at the center of the canvas, bringing into focus a nihilistic vision of the fate of chimpunity. After Busner and Jane Bowen attend the opening of Dykes's latest exhibition, Busner then goes to a Covent Garden opera. That he finds this production less aesthetically appealing than his patient's show points out his distrust of middle-class attitudes. Rather than concentrating on his old friend Peter Wiltshire's production of *Turandot,* Busner reflects on Dykes's apocalyptic paintings, noting a correspondence between Dykes's method and his own psychoanalytic methods as he realizes how much the paintings impressed him:

The idea of depicting, allegorically, the anti-naturalism of the condition of modern urban chimpunity appealed to him. What Dykes was doing with imagery was, he felt, similar to his own search for a psycho-physical approach to neurological and psychiatric disorders. The bodies of the chimps in Dykes's paintings were placed in destructive environments—a crashing plane, a burning escalator, a plague-struck furniture superstore—which could be seen as analogues of the distorted relation between chimps' minds and chimps' bodies. (185–86)

Busner's interpretation of the paintings attempts to plumb deeper into their symbolic significance than the comments George Levinson, Dykes's gallery agent, offers. Levinson provides a pretentious and trendy reading of Dykes's subject matter, identifying the paintings' subject as "the body of the archetypal chimp constrained, crushed and distorted by the pressures of modern, urban life" (182). Self embeds between these two readings Simon Dykes's own understanding of the importance of his recent paintings, filtering the artist's thoughts through the omniscient narrator. Dykes tries to link his artistic preoccupations with his delusion, noting that "the content of these hallucinations, these delusions of the bestial masking the human, were made up, constructed from the materials of his own mordant obsessions. What, after all, were the apes, if not distorted versions of the body?" (183). These diverse attempts to comprehend the implications of the paintings' imagery reveal the various characters' self-interested interpretations, pointing out the correlation between exegesis and subjectivity.

When Simon Dykes contemplates the effects on a painter of the loss of perspective, he intimates that the boundaries between an artist's life and work are indistinguishable. If his paintings express his corporeal anxieties, they also provide a key to his recovery: the image of the infant propelled through space. One perplexing obstacle he runs up against in the early stages of his recovery is the unshakeable belief that he has three sons rather than two. Jean Dykes denies that there had ever been a Simon Jr. as he claims, but Simon eventually learns that he had adopted a pet human in a program run by the London Zoo. Along with a television crew, Dykes and Busner travel to Africa where the human youth had been returned to the wild and given the nickname Biggles. After seeing Biggles in the wild Simon tells Busner that the boy "looked just like any other human to me, nasty, brutish and long of leg" (403).

As with his fictional oeuvre as a whole, in *Great Apes*, Self dramatizes his own version of J. G. Ballard's conception of "inner space," which Ballard describes as "that psychological domain . . . where the inner world of the mind and the outer world of reality meet and fuse."[10] For Dykes, this constitutes a chasm between his subjective reality and the external reality, with his madness viewed in terms of transgressing the conventions and standards of rational thoughts and behavior. Once Dykes has come to terms with his chimpunity under Busner's guidance, at the novel's closing, Busner poses to him a new interpretation of Dykes's complex human delusion, placing it "more in the manner of a satirical trope" (404). Since satire depends greatly on the reader's ability to ultimately recognize the principal subject that the author ridicules or attacks, Self draws his fictional universe in such a way that its complements in the actual world rarely remain deeply submerged beneath the novel's surface. This method lends further support to the novel's verisimilitude, allowing for suspension of disbelief amid this surreal and absurdist fictive domain.

It has become commonplace to claim that a writer chronicles her or his respective zeitgeist, yet the axiom applies substantially to Self. His fiction deflates the pretensions inherent within various contemporary milieus, and part of his comic as well as satiric efficacy stems from his uncompromising manner of placing aggrandizing claims of value into critical perspective. Self's fiction attempts to convey the texture and attitudes of the contemporary world much in the same way that in *Flat Pack Stops at Ebola* Simon Dykes is said to have "caught the feel of an aisle at the Swedish furniture supermarket, Ikea, perfectly" (178). By creating characters and scenes that resemble actual people and places, as individuals and composites, Self intensifies the matrix of relationships between his fiction and actuality. Many real-life cultural personalities are detectable in these characters, some of whom are identified explicitly while others have been transformed into characters. The Oxford anthropologist Redmond O'Hanlon, author of travelogues including *In Trouble Again,* appears as the marijuana-smoking naturalist Raymond Hamble, author of a book about the Amazon entitled *In Deep Shit* (331); Lloyd Grossman, presenter of the BBC series *Masterchef,* and the chef Anton Mosiman appear as Lloyd Grosschimp and Anton Mosichimp respectively (376). Elsewhere topical references to Bill Clinton, the O. J. Simpson trial, the death of the playwright John Osborne, and others provide additional clues to the novel's temporal setting, 1995—the center of what Self has frequently referred to as a period of decadence.

This decadence cannot be reduced to mere hedonism, though profligacy in many forms rarely strays far from the overall decadence. Commenting on the 1990s in a review of a cultural history of the decade, Self writes that "in so far as this decade had any character at all, it was the merest trace of *maquillage,* dabbed across the awful, ravaged face of decadence."[11] In other words, despite the attempts at altering the surface, or the period's outward aspect, the 1990s strongly resemble the fin de siécle from the previous century—a point Self depicts at length in his novel *Dorian*. The bestial face that so horrifies Simon Dykes as he looks at his lover, Sarah, or at any of the other chimps inhabiting London is in effect his true nature masked by the synthetic products of his era. In this respect the human-to-chimpanzee transformation does indeed provide a satirical trope, as Busner remarks to Dykes at the end of the novel, one that encompasses the intellectual narcissism inherent in humans attempting to separate themselves from the animal world. Such beliefs become predicated on a form of relativism, itself a hallmark of the late twentieth century.

Responding to an interviewer's question about Self's religious beliefs, asking whether he was an atheist, Self replied that through his recovery from drug and alcohol addiction he learned the benefit of healthy skepticism. "I have to go back to agnosticism, to the luxury of doubt," Self replied. "If I allow myself the luxury of doubt in this area, I am wholly conflicted. All my study of religion leads me to believe that there is a hell of a lot more to religious belief than the notion that it is simply an opiate."[12] With *How the Dead Live*, Self presents the after-death experience of a confirmed atheist confronting the reality she so strenuously denied throughout her adult life. More introspective than any of his previous works, *How the Dead Live* combines aspects of Self's personality with that of his mother while expanding the central conceit of "The North London Book of the Dead" to imagine death from the mother's point of view.

As with the responses to his previous works, reviewers of *How the Dead Live* divided sharply in the opinions of the novel's merits, but even when disagreeing on the ultimate quality of the book, several critics evoked James Joyce's *Ulysses* as a reference point. Writing in the *Guardian,* Elaine Showalter observed that "what *How the Dead Live* lacks in economy of structure it repays in lavishness of feeling and characterisation. Lily is a colossal heroine, a nighttown Molly Bloom who memorably reveals herself through her furious monologue. What begins as a satiric novel of ideas ends as a surprisingly moving elegy."[13] Tom Shone points out that the novel "consists of a monologue by a Jewish mother who goes by the name of Bloom. So naturally, the first thing you do upon picking up the book is flick to the final page to see what the last word is. And sure enough, instead of 'yes'—the word used by James Joyce to end 'Ulysses'—we find the contemporary negative 'Not,' as used by Mike Myers in his canonical postmodern masterpiece, 'Wayne's World.'"[14] As Shone states, the similarity between Lily Bloom's name and that of Joyce's antiheroine suggests that Self might have been alluding to *Ulysses,* an unsurprising gesture given Self's typical allusiveness in his fiction. Nevertheless, in a radio interview Self refuted such suggestions, declaring that he had read only half of *Ulysses.*[15] Instead Self pointed out that the name is fortuitous, deriving from his maternal grandmother, Lillian Rosenbloom. One additional source for this image-laden surname is Bloom's kosher restaurant in Golders Green, where Elaine Self took her sons in an expression of her Jewish roots.[16] The question of nominal allusions ignores the fact that "Lily Bloom" is a germane and imagistic name.

Figuratively encoded within Lily's name, the motifs of death and rebirth traditionally associated with Easter and spring comprise two aspects of the novel's depiction of an afterlife, but in line with the personal nature of *How the Dead Live* such images can also convey the ironic dimensions of Self's feelings. He has written about his antipathy toward the Christian holiday and his mother's death: "My mother died at Easter. She who thought all religion was an out-and-out con, in that beautifully wiseacre fashion only a native New Yorker can achieve. She died in the Royal Ear Hospital of lung cancer—an irony which she might have appreciated, were it not for the fact that, in dying, my mother was fearful, alone, angry and devoid of any humour, no matter how black."[17] In *How the Dead Live* this anger becomes Lily Bloom's prime rhetorical characteristic, in conjunction with her profanity, as she rants about her children, husbands, society, and life itself. The novel contains significant sympathy and tenderness as well as irony and satire. Like the narrator of "The North London Book of the Dead," the short story that provides the fictive origin of the novel, Self has recounted how after his mother's death he would see phantom images of her:

> In mourning my mother—whom I loved very deeply—I went through all the recognised stages of anger, denial and eventual acceptance. Like the disciples, in the days and weeks immediately succeeding her death I would see "fake" mothers wandering the streets of London much as she did in life. However, since neither of us believed remotely in the existence of personal immortality (and she in no kind of transcendence whatsoever), these visitations were mute and hazy. If Mother had felt driven to communicate anything to me from beyond the grave, it would doubtless have been a sardonic remark about the cost of her cremation.[18]

Lily shares Elaine Self's rigid atheism, creating a situational irony in the novel as she confronts the realities of immortality. Her materialist view of the world, one to which she obstinately clings in death, has in this regard been proven to be in error.

In this image of Lily's death Self draws from various mythological sources, mixing eastern and western beliefs. Contemporary variations on the ancient Greek conception of Hades, the *Egyptian Book of the Dead,* and other belief systems proliferate throughout the novel, but no single source seems as significant as the *Bardo Thödol* or *Tibetan Book of the Dead.* While Joyce patterned *Ulysses* on Homeric myth, Self takes the *Tibetan Book of the Dead* as his template for his fictional afterlife. Divided into four distinct sections—"Epilogue," "Dying," "Dead," and "Deader"—and with an italicized section headed "Christmas 2001" that closes the epilogue and each of the chapters in the "Dead" and "Deader" sections, *How the Dead Live* presents life as karmic and potentially cyclical, dispelling rational linearity. At its essence the plot of the novel, though, is straightforward, progressing from April 1988 to Christmas 2001, thematically playing off the traditional Christian holidays of Jesus Christ's death and resurrection and birth. As the novel opens, Lily Bloom lies dying in London's Royal Ear Hospital, and the novel then follows her through the course of her indoctrination into London's dead, "living" as she does in a suburb called Dulston, and she continues to observe her two daughters while carrying on an existence not that different from life. At the close of the novel she has been reincarnated as the daughter of Natasha, Lily's youngest daughter and a heroin addict. Along the way she supplies details of her life in the United States and England, and she is accompanied by Rude Boy, David Kaplan, Jr.,[19] her son who died aged nine in 1957, when Lily was living in Vermont, and by Lithy, the lithopedion or calcified fetus that Lily miscarried in the 1960s. Lily's death guide, an Australian aborigine named Phar Lap Jones—whose name alludes to the famous New Zealand thoroughbred of the 1930s—guides her transition into death. A representative of traditional belief systems other than monotheism, Phar Lap serves as the steward of Lily's soul.

Appearing at Lily's bedside as she dies, Phar Lap provides Lily with her first instructions regarding death. "None of this is real, Lily," he tells her. "None of Lily is real. None of it ever has been. Dump your Lilyness now, girl. It doesn't suit you. Dump it or go round in it again like a set of old clothes."[20] But Lily does not "geddit," as Phar Lap implores; the karmic consequences of her thoughts during this critical moment as she enters the Buddhist primary Clear Light are lost upon her, just as they are as she undergoes her *Bardo* state, the transitional period in Buddhist belief that begins immediately after the moment of death. The *Tibetan Book of the Dead* reveals that an early *Bardo* stage involves karmic illusions, aural and visual hallucinations that can terrify the newly deceased. For Lily one of the most startling illusions is a group of entities known as the Fats, assemblages of all the weight she has lost and gained through her years of dieting. "It's not scary—it's terrifying, yet oddly pathetic as well," Lily remarks of her first encounter with the Fats. "They're disgustingly obese versions of me, all wobble and jounce, huge dewlaps of belly dangling to their knees. They've no eyes, hair or nipples, and they've the slack mouths I last saw on my own corpse. They're the Pillsbury Dough girls of total dissolution" (179). The Fats are not the only false images that Lily confronts. Because the novel takes place during her *Bardo* existence, all that she experiences is illusory. As Phar Lap tells Lily shortly after she attends her first Personally Dead meeting—a group support session as part of a twelve-step program for the recently deceased—it is all in her head: "None of it's real. None of it at all—you, me, this, whatever. . . . It's you who're no-thing. Recognise it an' all this . . . this guna will evaporate" (201). Lily believes in these illusions partly because they jibe so well with her expectations and also because of their level of detail. Such reasoning exemplifies the thrust of Self's narrative strategies.

How the Dead Live connects to Self's other work in several ways. As with all of his major works of fiction, there are direct textual bridges to other novels and stories. In addition to the thematic correspondence to "The North London Book of the Dead," Self points to his previous work by giving Jane Bowen, Zack Busner's colleague at Heath Hospital, a minor role in the novel. The novel also offers a parallel for Self's view of fiction. Essentially, the world that Lily constructs while refusing to relinquish her conscious selfhood creates an alternate universe, much in the way that Self constructs a parallel world for the actual one that his readers inhabit. Lily does not disbelieve what she sees because of the textures of minutiae that instill verisimilitude, combing the quotidian and extraordinary. This juxtaposition of the mundane and fantastic provides the foundation of what Self describes as his "dirty magical realism," a type of fiction that simultaneously embodies the bizarre and the familiar. Not only do Lily's death experiences approximate those in her life, if perhaps even a bit duller, she and the other residents of necropolitan London conform in terms of behavior and personality—including prejudices, most strikingly Lily's Jewish anti-Semitism—to how they lived. Even the objects that the dead maintain are the same from life, emphasizing the continuity between life and death.

As in life, the dead also have their celebrities; Laurence Olivier, Robin Cook (Derek Raymond), A. J. Ayer, R. D. Laing, and other real-life figures have cameos in the novel. Such pairings create a sense of credibility, encouraging the reader to suspend disbelief like Lily, while also serving at times comic and thematic purposes. Derek Raymond's appearance in the novel is Self's homage to the author of the "Factory" series of crime novels, the fifth of which is also titled *How the Dead Live* (1993). Ayer, Lily points out, clearly enjoys his "phantom existence" in the afterlife, and she speculates "that only such a relentless rationalist could gain any succour from these, the nervous tics of the afterlife" (251). Whereas *My Idea of Fun* marks Self's first detailed exploration of his "dirty magical realism," *How the Dead Live* is the novel in which he begins to maximize the style's narrative potential.

For all its attention to universal considerations, the novel remains Self's most personal work, and he imbues Lily with many of his mother's own characteristics. While Lily resembles Elaine Self physically, she also shares with her a pronounced strain of Jewish anti-Semitism. Self has written about his mother's conflicting feeling of their Jewish heritage: "This was the identity she retailed me, one made up in equal parts of Semophilia and that most corrosive of anti-Semitisms: Jewish anti-Semitism. . . . I have always been in the peculiar position of being freighted with an identity by two, violently opposed groups; groups that have been internalised within my own psyche."[21] Lily and her daughters show no compunctions in renaming a shop "Jewmar" from its original "Lewmar"—the name deriving from those of the owners, Lewis and Mary Rubens—as a display of their "anti-Semitic wits" (54).[22] She believes retrospectively that she married her first husband, Dave Kaplan (who claimed to have changed his name from Carter in order to appear Jewish), because of his Jewish anti-Semitism (78). As Lily says of Hitler's presumed Jewishness, "surely *only* a Jew could hate Jews with such intensity, wish to rip out the kike sleeved within the Jew" (78). In a passage that provides a catalogue of cultural references that help to sum up the early 1990s, Lily ends her litany of nihilistic and racist remarks by stripping Woody Allen—an early inspiration for Self—of all distinguishing features except for those that strike her as stereotypical of a Jewish man, reducing him simply to a type: "And another clever, famous, Jewish wiseacre fought another million-dollar suit against the shiksa he'd discarded in favour of her adopted child. Oy-oy-oy gevalt!" (298).

While such statements do not wholly define Lily, they efficaciously depict her as a complex and conflicted character—one who earns the reader's sympathy, however distasteful and offensive she might seem at moments, through her frank confessions. Lily's anti-Semitism reveals itself to be an intense manifestation of not simply self-hatred or self-denial but her distaste for life, resulting from a string of bitter disappointments from her childhood to her children. *How the Dead Live* is a tragic example of a posthumous communion between son and mother, a belated Kaddish, the Judaic prayer of mourning, that preserves the mother's soul. The novel depicts several souls in crisis, and just as Phar Lap aids Lily in fighting for her own soul she wants to do the same for her youngest daughter, Natasha.

Self's harshest characterization concerns Natasha, who as a heroin addict loses all dignity. By viewing his two-decades-long addiction to drugs and alcohol through the lens of a female character, Self gains a measure of critical distance from his personal problems, which had already been available for public scrutiny. Whereas *Great Apes* was published amid the controversy of the shambles involving Self's dismissal from the *Observer*, with *How the Dead Live* he places his history of drug and alcohol addiction into critical perspective. Like Self, Natasha Yaws was born in 1961,[23] and her life takes her down avenues similar to those

Self traversed during his years of addiction. Self has stated that substance abuse thwarted his own dignity and that "I actually found I was doing things that were against my moral will, not just occasionally, but a lot of the time, on a daily basis."[24] A junkie, Natasha likewise displays a negated moral will by placing her need for heroin above all other considerations. Because of her enslavement to heroin addiction, Natty—as Lily refers to her in a reminder that Natasha remains childlike in many respects while also implying that she has become physically dilapidated and emotionally decadent—has capitulated to defeat in the fight for her own soul. This psychomachic parallel between mother and daughter reinforces the novel's depiction of death as another existential stage rather than a terminus by hinting at the karmic implications of one's actions in life.

Beautiful and intelligent, Natasha uses her natural gifts and charms to manipulate the people closest to her in order to sate her narcotic needs. Although her sister, Charlotte, outwardly seems more the materialistic and pragmatic sibling, where drugs are concerned Natasha surpasses her sister's acquisitiveness and resorts to Machiavellian ploys to obtain them, heedless of the cost to others. While callously exploiting his feelings to obtain what she wants from him, she remains indifferent to Miles, who sleeps with her after she receives an afternoon pass from a rehabilitation facility near Reigate (263–64). She then meets her dealer and partner, Russell, for an emotionally sterile coupling. The successive sexual encounters create uncertainty regarding the paternity of Natasha's baby. Although Natasha undergoes costly rehabilitation therapy at a clinic called Pullet Green, Lily remarks that "you could take the drugs and booze out of Natty, but the addiction to the power of her own private place remained as deep and smooth and moist as the orifice itself.

Nope, all they did at Pullet Green—all they *could* do—was to dry her out, set her up, and send her out again" (260–61). At various points in the novel, in chapters set in both London and Australia, Natasha surreptitiously takes her dying mother's diamorphine, descends to prostitution, neglects her daughter, and carries out a host of other actions linked directly to her addiction. While those around her, such as Miles, suffer, her own emotions have become blunted. Natasha displays such an overwhelming absence of affect that Delilah, her toddler and Lily's reincarnated form, refers to her as the Ice Princess. While succinctly capturing Natasha's indifference to others, the appellation also calls to mind the novel's recurring ice cream metaphors. Lily's adult fondness for ice cream provides a link to one of the pleasant aspects of her emotionally troubled childhood, and after her death she takes a job writing press releases at a company called Baskin's, a probable reference to the ice cream chain Baskin-Robbin's to which she directly refers when discussing first Yehudi Menuhin and then her cancer surgery (83).

The italicized chapter codas compound the tragedy of Natasha's addiction and Lily's determination to be reborn as her own granddaughter. As these sections progress on Christmas thirteen years after Lily's death, Delilah, now an eighteen-month-old toddler, is left to fend for herself alone in house with no food or electricity. Natasha and Russell have died of heroin overdoses—she in bed, he on the kitchen floor. The only food available to Delilah is a piece of Christmas cake, left tantalizingly out of her reach; this forces her to lick icing from Russell's mouth and forage for crumbs while also drinking from a toilet. One small consolation is that she is able to smoke cigarettes someone has left behind, an image that connects *How the Dead Live* to the ending of *My Idea of Fun,* where the Fat Controller, reborn as Ian Wharton's son, smokes cigars. Knowing that she will die of either starvation or hypothermia, Delilah considers and then rejects suicide. Inspired by an actual case of a toddler that died under similar circumstances, Self captures the stark consequences of drug addiction by writing from the perspective of the child, albeit here a toddler in full possession of an adult consciousness. At the same time, he intensifies the novel's poignancy and existential (if not fatalistic) circularity. Lily/Delilah addresses these passages to her only companion, Natasha's lithopedion, who appeared from Natty's bed when she died three days earlier. Asking what one can expect from a lithopedion, Delilah answers her own question with a string of negatives, positing that her codas and by extension the entire novel functions as both a Jewish prayer of remembrance, Yizkor, and as a memento mori: "Nothing much. No-thing. Except this: forget me. Not" (404).

Several novels in recent years explore the effects of death on the human body. In Jim Crace's *Being Dead* (1999), for example, a couple journey to the secluded beach that provided the setting for their first sexual experience together decades before; however, instead of recapturing their younger life, they are murdered. The novel then thoroughly describes the disintegration of their corpses. Another journey figures prominently in Graham Swift's *Last Orders* (1996) as a man's closest friends and son carry his cremated remains from London to Margate in order to fulfill his final wish. This pervasive thread in contemporary literature of depicting corpses in unidealistic terms, a practical agnostic response to corporeal anxieties, lends the impression of a postmortem era rising from the shade of postmodern experimentation. These universal concerns cross multiple boundaries, including time and medium, and like Martin Amis's existential mystery novel, *Other People* (1981), as well as filmmaker David Lynch's equally cyclical *Mulholland Drive, How the Dead Live* transcends material considerations to explore prime metaphysical enigmas.

Great Apes and *How the Dead Live* each deal in their respective ways with battles for identity and a person's soul, but rather than straightforwardly personifying abstract concepts such as good and evil as do works typically associated with psychomachia, Self instead places these elements in the everyday world. Even though *How the Dead Live* is ostensibly narrated from the afterlife, because Lily's illusive visions of death so closely mirror ordinary life Self's "dirty magical realism" achieves its most powerful expression to date. When set against the author's highly publicized problems with drug and alcohol addiction, these novels also reflect the battle Self waged for his own soul and identity as a father, son, husband, and novelist.

CHAPTER EIGHT

"Here and There, Now and Then"

Dorian: An Imitation, Dr Mukti and
Other Tales of Woe, and The Book of Dave

"So what if the whole giddy rondo had the air of the *fin de siè-cle* about it," asks the implied author near the close of *Dorian* (2002). "Because it *was* the end of the twentieth century, and after a hundred years of willed decline, there was a feeling abroad in the land that things could only get better."[1] For a novel that opens with an epigraph taken from Arthur Schopenhauer's *Studies in Pessimism,* it is no surprise that as *Dorian* concludes, this note of brusque optimism should stem from a collective acknowledgement of self-imposed social degeneration. Rather than a will to live, the characters in Dorian embody a nihilistic compulsion. Will Self reworks Oscar Wilde's only novel as a satiric demonstration of the synergetic affinity of the two end-of-the-century periods, giving the twentieth century a cyclical aspect.

Long an admirer of Wilde's writing, particularly *The Portrait of Dorian Gray* (1891), Self fittingly turns to this salient fin de siécle text in order to capture the overarching characteristics he sees in the 1980s and '90s. Early in the centennial year of Wilde's death, Self wrote that he was reworking this seminal Decadent novel by moving it forward a century: Wilde's "observations of social mores, the melodrama of debauched morals and the superlative epigrams, which apotheosise *everything,* all remain as fresh as the day they were penned."[2] Self has repeatedly insisted that decadence characterizes the contemporary zeitgeist; the 1990s in particular, he argues, "existed in dyadic relationships with two other decades, the 1980s—for which they were a rerun with knobs on, sort of: '1980s (R)'—and the 1890s."[3] Although Self originally adapted Wilde's novel into a screenplay, modeling his script on Bruce Robinson's *Withnail & I,* as he neared its completion he decided instead to turn his script into a novel, which allowed him to retain creative control.[4] Subtitled "An Imitation," Self's *Dorian* takes Wilde's text as its template, and Self explicitly develops the homoerotic themes at which Wilde could only hint.

While essentially faithful (until the epilogue) to Wilde's novel, Self makes significant alterations to emphasize the continuity of the two works' respective eras. The central image in Wilde's novel, Basil Hallward's painting of Dorian, becomes in Self's version a video installation—*Cathode Narcissus*—consisting of nine monitors, all displaying youthful Dorian's naked figure to impart a sensation of "the most intense, carnivorous, predatory voyeurism" (12). Hallward views *Cathode Narcissus* as his swansong in the medium, one that "was *born* decadent, like all the rest of conceptual art. First it was Nauman, then Viola and me, now it's finished. From now on, conceptual art will degenerate to the level of crude autobiography" (13). Self targets contemporary artists such as Tracey Emin and Gavin Turk, much in the way that he pokes fun at the 1990s London art milieu in *Great Apes.* Just as the painting in Wilde's novel comes to reveal Gray's moral dissolution by manifesting the physical degradations to which Gray is immune—a metaphor for syphilis— *Cathode Narcissus* likewise exhibits the protagonist's decadence by displaying the various stages of HIV and AIDS; even the installation's videocassettes eventually succumb to decay. By replacing the original canvas and oil with video monitors and cassettes for Hallward's contemporary portrait of Dorian Gray, Self constructs a metaphor rich in symbolic connotations: Gray inhabits a pixilated society, one in which the illusion of youth can be preserved onscreen through television and film media. "Everyone who isn't a pseudo-intellectual loves television—it's so much *realer* than reality," the narrator claims (66), a view that Henry Wotton mimics when claiming that Dorian and Princess Diana are both actors and that "they find acting so much more *real* than reality" (108). Immodestly perhaps, Self has pointed out the continuities between Wilde's era and his own by declaring that "*The Picture of Dorian Gray* is the prophecy and *Dorian* is the fulfilment."[5]

Neil Bartlett, the *Guardian*'s reviewer of the novel and author of two Wildean pastiches, proclaims that Self's transpositions of Wilde's material "illuminate both the historic original and their contemporary setting; they are also, shamelessly, fun."[6] Self takes other liberties with his primary source material by intensifying its thematic scope, which Bartlett views as appropriate for the both the novel's late-twentieth-century setting and for Self's narrative style:

Of course, this being the 20th not the 19th fin de siecle, and Self being the writer he is, he ups both the body count and the sexual explicitness. In the original Dorian is accused of virtually every crime, but is never actually nailed as a sodomite. In Self's version Wilde's dark hints are elaborated into full-blown and fully enacted queerness (of several accurately detailed varieties) for all the protagonists. In addition, where the original limits addictions to cigarettes and opium, Self supplements these primitive pleasures with a pharmacopoeia of class A drugs. His narrator lavishes a pornographer's breathless exactitude on the physical practicalities of intoxication; in several exhilarating passages not only the prose but even the narrative itself swoons, lurches and tumesces in a brilliantly realised simulacrum of chemical derangement. [7]

These are hardly the extent of Self's textual alterations. He transforms Dorian Gray's fiancée, Sybil Vane, into a homeless, black male prostitute and drug addict named Herman. James Vane, Sybil's brother in the original, appears in Self's version as Ginger, an unpleasant skinhead and Herman's lover. Whereas Wilde deals coyly with homoeroticism and what the English psychologist Havelock Ellis termed "sexual inversion"—as a corrective to Richard von Krafft-Ebing's theories of homosexuality as perversion—Self presents his characters' homosexuality frankly, depicting a society in which privileged men and women storm from their previously closeted worlds.

As Basil Hallward explains to Lord Henry Wotton, Gray "belongs to a totally new generation, the first gay generation to come out of the shadows" (12). While clearly faithful to their incarnations in Wilde's novel, Baz Hallward and Henry Wotton embody two distinct perceptions of gay identity among the generation slightly older than Gray's own. Hallward, an activist manqué and proselytizer for gay rights, possesses a "pink militancy" (40), while the married Wotton remains ambivalent about his sexual preference and rejects "gay" as a term of sexual identification (40). Dismissing Wilde's famous declaration that Wotton, Hallward, and Gray represent respectively his public image, self-image, and ideal image as "a meaningless remark" and noting that in *The Picture of Dorian Gray* Wotton is very much Wilde, Self states that his updated Wotton "is one part me and two other parts people I knew who fitted the bill." [8]

Self has claimed that in writing his novels he becomes at times wholly absorbed by his material, going to such extents as swinging from tree branches and pant-hooting while writing *Great Apes*. He admits to similar—if more vicarious—preoccupations in writing *Dorian*.

> Like most novelists I am broadly shallow. When I was writing a novel about chimpanzees I became fixated by the debate about animal rights, when I was writing one about attitudes to mortality I became enthralled by Tibetan Buddhism. For the past year or so I've been "rewriting" Dorian Gray, setting it in the time of AIDS and the "liberated" milieu Wilde anticipated. Predictably, during the writing I've become obsessed with issues surrounding sexuality. In my experience sexual orientation is mutable, and in working my way into the minds of my same-sex loving protagonists, I found myself enjoying enhanced homosexual fantasies.[9]

Self's aside helps to situate his discussion on the semantic utility of "gay" as a descriptor for same-sex relationships. "I've also been having the debate about sexuality that I thought AIDS might provoke—the debate about the redundancy of 'gay,'" he continues in this article, an essay that appeared at the same time as *Dorian* and seems intended to help promote the novel.[10]

Like Wotton, Self considers "gay" dubious as an identifying term for same-sex relationships. "Let's face it," Self writes in "Identity Crisis," the word has "been semantically twisted and bent over the years until its connotations are at best fluffily innocuous—some might even say specious—and at worst hopelessly contraindicated."[11] Some critics have been equally suspicious of Self's appropriation of queer politics for his novel. Richard Canning, reviewing *Dorian* in the *Independent*, condemns what he sees as the novel's "rictus sneer" and takes additional umbrage with "its cheap flippancy concerning AIDS, and its hostile prurience towards homosexuality. This novel is more mired in the selfish misanthropy of the 1980s than its author understands."[12] Early in the second section of the novel, Baz Hallward repeats theories concerning the possibility of HIV lying dormant in the liberated years "between the Stonewall Riots and the arrival of AIDS" (94) but that the hedonism of this era and its attendant "ever lengthening conga line of sodomy" (95) created a new form of enslavement. "Simple to observe that for men who were meant to be free," he says, "how readily they draped themselves in chains" (95).

Covering a period of sixteen years, *Dorian* begins in the summer of 1981, one month before Prince Charles and Diana Spencer's heavily promoted wedding, at the beginning of a "tidal wave of debauchery" (54). At Dorian's *vernissage,* the debut of both his video installation and of Herman, the attendees share a hypodermic needle to inject drugs before assembling into "a conga line of buggery" (68). *Dorian* combines satire with a foreboding fatalism, and Self tithes the fates of Princess Diana and the queer community, yoking them together through AIDS as the setting moves forward a decade. While Wotton—hospitalized on an AIDS ward that Princess Diana and the United States' First Lady, Barbara Bush, had just visited—refuses to "kowtow to the Windsors" (108) and denotes the Princess of Wales through contemptuous epithets such as "Fatty Spencer" (80), "Her Royal Regurgitation," and "The Princess of Clothes" (108), Dorian Gray recognizes himself in her. Wotton tells Baz Hallward that Dorian has an affinity with the Princess Diana and that "Dorian's intent on being the ultimate fag—and she's the ultimate fag hag" (108). More crucial, Wotton credits his former protégé for understanding "how her particular act—her grazed heart crying out for a Band-aid, while she shops 'til every last equerry drops—constitutes the very *Zeitgeist* itself" (108). Both become totemic icons for a superficial, image-focused era, a period of decadence that neither survives.

A creature of image and will, Dorian is able to blend chameleonlike into any social setting from the circle of homosexual men gathered around the Princess of Wales to the leather bars in the bowels of Manhattan's meat-packing district. At times he stands at the vanguard of image trends, giving the impression of originating sartorial styles that other young gay men copied. But Dorian is, as Self told one interviewer, "a nasty little piece of work."[13] Like many of Self's previous characters, most noticeably Ian Wharton from *My Idea of Fun,* Dorian displays an overwhelming absence of empathy and sympathy for anyone else. However affected and pretentious his narcissistic attention to image make him, he exhibits a psychopathic lack of affect. In New York rumors circulate that "Dorian was the AIDS Mary, the malevolent and intentional transmitter of the virus" (112). Although immune from its effects—unlike *Cathode Narcissus*—Dorian is a carrier of HIV, and he gains sadistic ecstasy from infecting as many unsuspecting men and women as possible. While others take precautions to mitigate the transmission of the virus he enjoys practicing the most dangerous sexual acts as possible. His cruelty is psychological as well as physical, and as Baz Hallward recounts to Wotton, Dorian propelled his elder acquaintance back into depths of narcosis. Astutely conscious of his public persona, Dorian considers his actions and seems unable rather than unwilling to act impulsively. As he condescendingly brags to two young men, aping Wotton's penchant for epigrams and paradox, "I don't shudder to think—I think to shudder" (111).

In Wilde's novel, Dorian ruminates on his lifestyle and the legacy of his ancestors. His inheritance is not simply aristocratic; it strikes Dorian as essentially ontological, infusing the very core of his being. He believes that the past helps to compose future generations: "man was a being with myriad lives and myriad sensations, a complex multiform creature that bore within itself strange legacies of thought and passion, and whose very flesh was tainted with the monstrous maladies of the dead."[14] Self's Dorian Gray also inherits much from his ancestors—including, ironically, his father's homosexuality—but he takes even more from those around him. His contemporaries from Wotton and Hallward to those who fall victim to his lethal hedonism contribute to his collective legacy. In Self's novel HIV and AIDS render literal these "monstrous maladies of the dead" that taint Dorian's flesh, though it is of course *Cathode Narcissus* that initially bears its lesions and other marks. A *zeitroman,* or novel of its age, *Dorian* includes a textual soundtrack—pointing perhaps to its genesis as a film script—as a way of capturing the aura of its temporal setting. Early in the novel, for example, the pop group Soft Cell's "Tainted Love" provides an ironic foreshadowing of the AIDS crisis that ensues. "Had some strange poisonous germ crept from body to body till it had reached his own," Wilde's Dorian wonders, succinctly conveying the transmission of a lytic, or cell-destructive, virus. By literalizing Wilde's metaphors Self demonstrates the ways that the past and present coexist symbiotically, each imparting a rejuvenated appositeness to the other.

Self divides *Dorian* into three main narrative sections— "Recordings," "Transmission," and "Network"—plus an epilogue that by destabilizing its mimetic foundation alters the novel's entire fictional universe. Set in 1997, the epilogue opens with Dorian resurrected from his suicide in the previous chapter as he and Victoria "Batface" Wotton discuss the manuscript that Henry left behind—the novel itself to that point. *Dorian* carries clues to its metafictional element, as Wotton as putative author as well as character "plays with the form" (258): "Henry Wotton could have written a brilliant book about the life and times of . . . Henry Wotton, but as he himself said derisively, 'The only circumstances in which I would write a *roman à clef* would be if I lost my fucking car keys'" (41). As Victoria points out to Dorian, her late husband does in fact lose his keys on numerous occasions in the text (258).[15] To alleviate Dorian's concern about his harsh characterization in the novel, Victoria reminds him that it is fiction and that Wotton had taken pains to "formally distinguish" between the scenes in which he had privilege to details and those in which he did not (259). Self—or rather Wotton—achieves this by indicating dialogue in which Wotton directly participates (or is in the immediate vicinity) through the standard practice of inverted commas while signaling all other conversations through the typically European method of dashes. Notably, as Wotton dies and the jiggling man that had been meting out the seconds of Wotton's life like a human metronome ceases his Tourettic movements, his dialogue with this mysterious character is introduced through a dash (254–55).

While each of Self's novels contains some textual link to another work, *Dorian* looks both back to previous works and ahead to future ones. As the novel moves into the mid-1990s, it includes many of the same locations and characters as *The Sweet Smell of Psychosis,* "The Rock of Crack as Big as the Ritz," and "The Nonce Prize," all of which are set during this same period. Drug addiction's democratizing corollaries once again temporarily adjourn class distinctions as the novel moves from the Sealink Club in Soho (200–201) to the Chinaman's crack den on the Limehouse Causeway (208, 218). Further strengthening the connection to the London noir trilogy, Self gives brief cameos to Danny O'Toole, first going under the name of London, and for the third time in his fiction Self depicts him smoking crack at his fateful night at the Chinaman's house as Wotton conjures a scene of Dorian there as well.[16] In a thematic adjustment, Ginger instead of Mearns "thuds off down the stairs, elbowing aside two saddo boys sucking on a Volvic-bottle crack pipe" (219). Whereas Danny's presence hearkens to earlier work, Self also foreshadows his sixth novel, *The Book of Dave* (2006), through the character Cal Devenish. Dissolute through drug addiction in *Dorian,* Devenish began as a promising novelist, finding modest critical and popular success with his third novel, *Limp Harvest* (211). Devenish figures previously in Self's fiction as the judge for the prison creative-writing contest, the Wolfenden Prize that tightens the seal on Danny's fate in "The Nonce Prize." Physically—and at times verbally—resembling Self, he appears as an unsympathetic portrayal of Self's public persona during this same period. More importantly, this portrayal emphasizes Self's direct participation in this decadent milieu. As with Wilde's response to his characterizations of Dorian Gray, Henry Wotton, and Basil Hallward as three images of himself, Wotton and Devenish in *Dorian* embody two aspects of Self's own personas, which inevitably collide as Wotton in his dual capacity as character and self-reflexive author chides his counterpart. "You writers only ever pay attention to events so you can set fire to them during your paper ceremonials. . . . Whatever my faults, I have at least lived my life at first hand, rather than filtering it through this paper as part of a literary experiment" (220).

Like Wotton, Self adopts self-reflexive strategies throughout *Dorian,* drawing attention to the fictive method and the alternative world of Self's other fictional works. Although such intertextual techniques subvert the works' realist surface they can alter the readers' understanding of the actual world as well as its fictional analogue. "It's what I like to experience—a prickling at the back of the neck," he told one interviewer. "Not necessarily anything supernatural, but an ordinary reality being exposed as a construct. Or things not being what they seemed to be. That can be a reversal of people's cultural expectations or an undermining of their sense of what sanity is."[17] Cultural expectations and sanity both figure significantly into Self's following works.

In certain cases Self's short stories serve as prequels to his novels, introducing many of the themes and characters that he develops in more detail with the longer fiction. "The North London Book of the Dead" obviously foregrounds *How the Dead Live* much as "Inclusion®" sets the conditions for Simon Dykes's comprehensive delusions in *Great Apes*. Likewise, the emotos from "Caring, Sharing" and the ubiquitous "Davidity" of "Dave Too"—both from *Tough, Tough Toys for Tough, Tough Boys*—provide glimpses into the twinned historical periods of *The Book of Dave*. Self's fourth short story collection, *Dr Mukti and Other Tales of Woe* (2004), however, begins with a continuation of Zack Busner's ongoing story and ends with a coda to Self's second novel, *Great Apes*.

"Dr Mukti," the novella that constitutes the first half of the volume, follows the professional and personal rivalry between Busner and Shiva Mukti, a first-generation Indian immigrant. Their mutual animosity escalates from ethical transgressions to homicide, but it is Busner's and Mukti's individual hubris that lies behind the major events in the story.

A "psychiatrist of modest achievements but vaulting ambition,"[18] Mukti holds a consultancy appointment at St. Mungo's hospital, which for five years has been incorporated into the

Heath Hospital fold. Frustrated by his lack of professional advancement, the National Health Service, the disappointments in his personal life, and even in his continued friendship with a childhood schoolmate, David Elmley, Mukti is continually denied the respect for which he yearns. Self's fictional characters often appear as impotent entities whose fates lie in the hands of other forces. "Self-World," as reviewers have dubbed his alternative universe,[19] reminds its populace that they lack autonomy and that while free will might be an ameliorating concept it is simply an illusion. Mukti fits accordingly into this fictional milieu. His first and last names acknowledge respectively the Hindu destroyer god Shiva and the concept of *moksha*, or liberation from material concerns. The god Shiva exemplifies cosmic control, and is an effective analogue to the shaping forces that govern Self's fictional universe as one manifestation of an individual existing at the behest of another's fancy.

Deracinated from Varanasi, his ancestral homeland, and his family's Hindu and Brahaminic traditions, Mukti also loses faith in his profession. As he continues to be stymied in his desire for distinction in the psychiatric community Mukti grows increasingly paranoid and anti-Semitic, ultimately viewing Busner as the embodiment of the forces that impede his professional advancement. A specialist in schizophrenic disorders, even though his prime recourse for treatment is medication, Mukti eventually exhibits schizophrenic behavioral traits. For Mukti, Busner represents the basest aspects of the psychiatric profession, ultimately becoming the latter's personal bête noire, but even worse the elder psychiatrist represents a vital injustice. He holds the esteem that Mukti desires. One thought that Mukti resists formulating due to his anxiety of becoming mired in "stupefying bigotry" nevertheless places for him his and Busner's respective status into a clear perspective: "it was obvious that Busner was a Jew, and as such he must have access, if not to illuminati who ensured his advancement, at any rate to a number of sympathetic friends in very high places, who made certain that he maintained his position" (20). Despite the envious, bigoted nature of this explanation, it points out two significant problems. Members of minority groups often run up against discriminatory barriers in their desire for advancement in their professional or social standing, and Mukti typifies in this and other regards many of the cultural effects associated with postcolonialism. The passage also raises an important question: How does Busner manage to continue as a practicing psychiatrist, considering the extent of his ethical transgressions?

At the end of *Great Apes* the chimpanzee Zack Busner's medical license is suspended, implying that his career might be at an end. But he possesses a seemingly inexplicable resiliency. Approaching seventy, Busner continues to practice and even delivers a prestigious lecture at the Royal Society of Ephemera. His personal life, however, proves dispiriting as Charlotte, his second and significantly younger wife, conducts an affair while ostensibly attending conferences. Busner "couldn't unwish the children he'd had with Charlie, but if he could by some paradigm shift have managed to delete her from his life, he rather feared he might've done so" (69). One reviewer notes that Busner's domestic upheavals grants him a new aspect, observing that this "vision of Busner, abandoned by his second wife, struggling with arthritic fingers to prepare dinner for his young children, is sweet, recasting the magus as a broken, Bellovian figure."[20] Such transformations are essential to many of Self's characters but perhaps to Busner most of all.

Louis-Ferdinand Céline's *Journey to the End of Night,* an important early influence on Self's fiction, features a recurrent character, Robinson, who appears in seemingly implausible situations and historical moments. Self gleaned from Céline the marrying of vibrant prose to a naturalistic alternate fictional reality, and through Busner—the main Robinson-like figure of Self's oeuvre—he pays an allusive homage to Céline. Like the wandering Robinson, as he travels through Self's fictional world Busner helps to delineate the reality surrounding him.

Even though Mukti snubs him after Busner genially introduces himself at an affective disorder conference, Busner initiates what on the surface appears as a sign of professional regard. Mentioning a paper that Mukti published in the *British Journal of Ephemera,* a prominent publication in "Self-World," he refers a patient to Mukti for a second opinion. As the novella progresses, the psychiatrists enact a mutual exchange of patients, beginning with David "the Creosote Man" Juniper. The other psychotic patients they refer to one another include Gerald "Rocky" Neville, "a six-foot-seven would-be Rastafarian" (35) whose violent demeanor obscures the fact that he is "a conundrum walking around inside a banality" (37); Mohammed Kabir, an Army officer who claims to have been tortured by Mossad agents in Israel while working undercover as an MI6 operative to infiltrate terrorist groups; and Tadeuz Wadja ("Mr. Double"), a Polish émigré plagued by echolalia. Beneath the professional veneer of Busner and Mukti's "to-and-fro" (63) lies what Mukti believes to be a more sinister purpose.

In the Royal Society of Ephemera's lecture room, Mukti deduces that the conspiracy he had suspected all along held a more extensive reach than he previously imagined: "Just as Busner was intent on annihilating Mukti using psychotics as assassins, so the Praesidium of the Elders of Psycho-Zion was bent on controlling all of society, employing not only helpless isolated drones, but whole clusters of neurotic bomblets" (84). Instead of a "mere Semitic mutual advancement pact" Mukti becomes convinced that "theirs was a campaign of carpet bombing the culture with manufactured mental malaises" (84). These verbal and nominative images open like narrative wormholes to provide a portal between Self's fictional universe and the actual world. Self's readers cannot help but to detect in such passages the author's recognition of contemporary political tumult. While the martial imagery of Mukti's horrible epiphany also implies that the psychiatrist has psychological affinity with Kabir, the text retains an ambiguity regarding whether Mukti suffers from delusions or if he discovers the true nature of the psychiatric community in Self's fictional universe. Additionally, whether Mukti's death—murdered by Busner in the novella, suicide in *The Book of Dave*—brings his nightmares into the fictive reality or whether the final chapter of the novella is simply an extension of deliria, it remains appropriately prosaic.

Four short stories make up the remaining half of *Dr Mukti and Other Tales of Woe*. One prominent feature of these stories is that they reveal Self to be gradually expanding his fictive topography. As the subtitle implies, however, these stories contain an emotional as well as geographical affinity. The combination of these elements owes something to Self's abiding interest in psychogeography, which the French philosopher and social activist Guy Debord popularized in the 1950s and '60s.

"161"—the title refers to the number of a character's flat in a high-rise building—takes place, unusually for Self, in Liverpool. The story stems from Self's involvement with a project coordinated by the Liverpool Housing Action Trust in which eighteen artists and writers stayed and worked briefly in the soon-to-be-demolished Linosa Close tower block, in order to preserve some aspect of the community.[21] Centering on Carl, a semiliterate teenager fleeing a local gang led by a figure known as Twisted Gut, and Dermot O'Leary, an elderly widower, "161" is a bleak depiction of working-class lives. Knowing that Twisted Gut and his crew will kill him, Carl breaks into Dermot's flat in a desperate attempt to elude his vengeful pursuers. As Dermot goes about his daily life alone in the flat, Carl attempts to remain hidden and sneaks food when the older man goes to sleep. Because most have residents have already been relocated from the tower block and others like it, "leaving only puddles and smears of humanity" (135), gangs flourish, unimpeded in activities that include drug dealing, burglary, abduction, rape, and murder (135). But while the malefactors and the few remaining residents seem unable to forge any sort of connection, Carl and Dermot eventually discover an ephemeral communion through their enforced yet fortuitous intimacy. In an environment where human life contains little value such actions convey precious empathy.

"The Five-swing Walk" and "Conversations with Ord" are the first works of fiction that Self has set in or around Stockwell, the section of south London where he has lived since 1997. In addition to their expanded topography, these stories signify other recent developments in his writing. As with "161" and "Tough, Tough Toys for Tough, Tough Boys," which takes place in Scotland, both of these works acquire a fairly conventional narrative aspect. Less "dirty magical realism" than "dirty realism," these stories take few liberties with their mimetic facade, and the bleakness surrounding the characters' lives factors into the prose style. By setting aside puns and other verbal embellishments Self achieves a poignantly taut narrative sobriety.

In "The Five-swing Walk" a forty-six-year-old father takes his four children on an excursion through the playgrounds around their south London neighborhood, a reminder for the elder children of the happier and more secure time when their parents were married. As the story opens he dreams that his eldest son dies after being a hit by a taxi cab. Stephen, recently divorced from the mother of his three eldest children, lives in a cramped flat with his new partner and their eighteen-month-old daughter. For Stephen intimacy "is highly overrated" (187). The changes in his domestic life spring from an extramarital affair he had with his daughter's teacher, Miss Foster, and her resulting pregnancy. Filtered through Stephen's perspective, the story shuns intimacy between adults, which Self signals in part through the story's sense of anonymity. Stephen's surname is not disclosed —nor does he refer to his ex-wife or new partner by name, in thought or speech—and there is an impression that his life has been quickly imploding.

"All broke loose," the narrator presciently says of Stephen's transition between dreaming and awakening (185). Stephen takes his eighteen-month-old biracial daughter, Setutsi, to pick up his other three children from his former house, "a large detached Edwardian villa" (191) that materially reminds him of the discrepancy between his previous and current life. On their way there, Misfortune, a tragic personification, follows Stephen much in the way that the Fates dog Danny O'Toole in "The Nonce Prize." Set during a gray, autumn Saturday afternoon, which produces in Stephen an "aching weariness" by reminding him of the breakup of his marriage during this same season (197–98), "The Five-swing Walk" charts the rapidity with which tragedy enters into life. Indeed the story's title refers to how heartrending loss becomes when misfortune involves children. Melissa and Daniel, the oldest children, aged eight and six, want Stephen to take them and their younger siblings—Setutsi and two-year-old Josh—on the "four-swing walk" (197). Stephen comprehends their desire for this peripatetic excursion through local playgrounds: "The older children had come into consciousness on these four sets of swings: two in the local playing field, then one in an adjoining patch of overgrown park, and the last, tucked away in a playground on a council estate. Perhaps they hoped that if they swung high enough they could describe a perfect parabola into the past" (197).

The locations of these four sets of swings find accordance with the social geography of south London, growing increasingly isolated and detached from the children's regular experience. In addition the playgrounds themselves begin increasingly to manifest signs of neglect and vandalism, further analogues of Stephen's past and present situations. At the first location, "Melissa and Daniel left themselves behind as they swung, left behind their preternaturally aged selves, they travelled in time—if not space—to a place of fun, that was simply and physically now" (200). When they reach the end of this excursion at the council estate they encounter a black youth who ingratiates himself to the group. Stephen suspects that the seven-year-old Haile might not be entirely sane, though he seems harmless. After Daniel inadvertently wraps the chains of his swing around the crossbar of the swing, Haile climbs up to free them. Standing there he wraps the chains around his neck, "like some grotesquely chunky piece of jewellery" (212), before plunging to his death. As the story ends with Haile's legs kicking in air, propelling him on the "five-swing walk," a variation on Stephen's dream of the previous night is hideously transformed into reality, and his emotions break through the numbing barriers he has erected in his psyche.

Another journey through (and above) south London figures prominently into "Conversations with Ord." Whereas Self's earlier stories display a marked bias for first-person narrations, placing attention on the narrative act as well as on considerations of plot and characterization, "Conversations with Ord" is the only story in *Dr Mukti and Other Tales of Woe* featuring a first-person narrator. Like Stephen, this anonymous character is divorced following a sexual tryst, but as his wife tells him "it's not as if there were children involved" (228). The narrator's social life has become woefully diminished, reduced to a circle of three friends, only one of whom displays any affinity to the narrator. Keith, a former bank robber who was imprisoned during the 1970s and understands few cultural references pertaining to the decade, intermittently shared a lover with the narrator, a fact that accounts for "the nub of our friendship, and perhaps also the root of our dreary common isolation" (226).

"Conversations with Ord" correlates to Self's "PsychoGeography" column in that these two characters understand themselves largely in relation to their surroundings. As they walk through Vauxhall and other areas of south London, there is a firm connection between their lives and totemic buildings such as the Battersea Power Station, the CCTV cameras that pervade the city, the Thames, and other signifiers. Both "formidable mnemonists" (216), the narrator and Keith occupy themselves during their walks by playing two games: "mental Go-Chess," a game played on an imaginary board in which either player can arbitrarily alter the game from chess to Go (216), and an equally imaginary dialogue involving two characters of their own joint construction.

The first, Ord, is a Johnsonian character who holds authoritatively forth on a variety of topics. A brilliant octogenarian former army general and then wealthy business mogul, he is also obviously homosexual. A timeless if not ageless figure, Ord regales his Boswell with anecdotes of the early decades of the twentieth century and then discusses how much London has changed by the latter decades of the twenty-first century. Flambard, his "reticent biographer and amanuensis" (217), is in the narrator's opinion "like all biographers of the living, a ghoul standing by the side of the road his subject was to drive along, waiting for the inevitable crash so he could gawp and then write it down" (224). Both the narrator and Keith prefer inhabiting Ord's consciousness over Flambard's; more interestingly, their fictional constructs have over time acquired the illusion of actuality.

Ord and Flambard suggest an oblique commentary on Self's own fictive creations, and they typify certain aspects of the author-reader relationship in that their conversations privilege one side above the other. More importantly, the narrator and Keith have created these two figures—one dynamic, the other prosaic—as substitutes for the personal void in their lives. Their desire to bring the fictional and metaphorical into the literal culminates in the debate they decide to hold onboard a hot-air balloon. When their two companions—Bax, a washed-up novelist, and Sharon Crowd, the middle-aged woman who had been at various times all three men's lover—experience a failure of nerve the narrator and Keith decide instead on a game of mental Go, observing the similarity of London's topography to that of a game board. Understanding Keith's instructions to begin the game as Ord's command to leap from the balloon, some two hundred feet above the city, the narrator follows suit in a duly Flambardian fashion. Whether, as with *How the Dead Live,* the first-person narrator speaks from the afterlife or the ending—if not the entire story—results from the more surrealist realms of his psyche is left open, but as with so much of Self's fiction its Ballardian "inner space" frequently defies rational explanation.

The final story in *Dr Mukti* demonstrates the ways in which rationality and fictional reality are often out of sync. A coda to *Great Apes,* "Return to the Planet of the Humans" charts the psychic reentry into the human world from that of chimpanzees. Simon Dykes learns that he has experienced a delusion, "a fantasy built up out of satirical books and science-fiction films" (248–49). Set a few years after the events that *Great Apes* depicts, the story takes place in the contemporary moment, "a time of war and oppression" (255). But where the novel uses its satiric trope to place attention on animal rights, among other things, "Return" focuses directly on humans' lack of empathetic connection; the human world Simon reenters is a predominantly affectless milieu, a world of raging psychopathologies which acts as a foil for his delusions to show him as a creature possessing a crystalline rationality. Longing for the ape world he had come to love, Simon decides that he would have to paint it into existence, and that he might in the process "discover an idiom which would make it bearable to speak of being human" (254). At the end of the story Simon travels to Hampstead to see Busner, indulging in an ape fantasy amid the relative solitude of Hampstead Heath, psychically and morally alienated from human society.

As Stephen in "The Five-swing Walk" changes his daughter's diaper, he thinks of its future, "deposited in a landfill in the East Midlands, where it would wait for ten thousand years, to confront the perplexed archaeologists of the future with yet more evidence of their shit-worshipping ancestors" (189). This provocative image, as with other key elements from *Dr Mukti,* looks ahead to Self's fifth novel.

A bifurcated novel, *The Book of Dave* moves between its two distinct eras. Subtitled "a Revelation of the Recent Past and the

Distant Future," the novel splits its temporal setting. However, *The Book of Dave* remains rooted in the same geographical terrain across this temporal expanse, even though the landscape itself has altered substantially. Contemporary novelists frequently examine the present through historical perspective, turning to either the past or a prospective future as a means of exploring fundamental concerns about the individual and society. In his study *The Contemporary British Novel,* Philip Tew frames novelists' adoption of historicity as a return to myth, allegory, and parable. "This kind of reworking of long-established modes of narration," he writes, "in order to synthesize apparently irreconcilable qualities within the imaginary, marks out one major strand of contemporary novels that transform history, parable and myth into something contemporaneous."[22] While firmly planted in the present, Self's fiction often elucidates the present by satirizing aspects of the recent past.

Spanning 1988 to 2001, for instance, *How the Dead Live* provides among other things an astute summary of the 1990s as Lily Bloom rants about seemingly everyone and everything that characterize this period. Self's short story "The Indian Mutiny" and *My Idea of Fun* each show how the past continues to inform the present through the psychic burdens one acquires. In his recent work Self has become even more strenuously Janus-faced, looking backward and forward at the same time in order to explain the present. By dividing *The Book of Dave* into two distinct yet reflective periods, Self discovers a narrative strategy apposite to each of these temporal concerns.

In the first era, Self depicts a futuristic England—now referred to as "Ingerland," or simply as "Ing"—where a deluge and seven centuries of Davidity following the purported discovery of a text known as "The Book of Dave" have transformed the nation and

its customs. The country has atavistically regressed into dystopian feudalism, exacerbated by the misogynistic Puritan strain of
its most zealous Davidic adherents, who govern the country like
a bureaucratic Taliban. In the odd-numbered chapters set in
the future, which portray customs that the even-numbered chapters gradually and ironically explain, the chronology oscillates
through a period of some sixteen years. Likewise, the novel's
contemporary setting defies traditional temporal linearity. While
these chapters begin in December 2001 and conclude with
July 2003, the interceding sections portraying Dave Rudman's
personal travails move between 1987 and 2003. However,
in dismissing a conventionally chronological order, the novel's
narrative structure brings to light more meaningful forms of linearity.

At the center of the novel sits Dave Rudman, a frustrated,
depressed, and eventually insane London cabbie who has been
barred from seeing his son or entering within a one-mile
perimeter of the house his ex-wife shares with her new partner,
Cal Devenish, and Dave's son, Carl. Self's character names generally indicate some aspect of their identity or temperament,
and Dave Rudman clearly corresponds to other characters in
Self's oeuvre that share his first name. A lower-middle-class
English Everyman, Dave struggles with his own bitterness and
personal frustration, redeemed only in that, like his grandfather Benny Cohen, as a London cabbie Dave possesses the
Knowledge—the collection of the 320 routes through London,
which Dave imagines as a "plan" for a future version of the
city, New London. Dave's lineage extends through Self's entire
fictional corpus, from Jim Stonehouse in "Waiting," the final
story in *The Quantity Theory of Insanity,* to Stephen in "The
Five-swing Walk."

The eponymous tome is a volatile black rant, the culmination of Dave's myriad angers. In this book he lashes out at seemingly everyone who has hindered him in some fashion: among them his ex-wife, Michelle; their lawyers; Cal Devenish, his ex-wife's new partner; the Child Support Agency; the Public Carriage Office (the PCO, which in the future sections becomes a menacing "priestly hierarchy"); and "flyers," those passengers Dave ferries to and from Heathrow. Although Dave's vitriol dampens eventually after the semicathartic process of writing and then burying the book—which he has professionally (and expensively) printed on metal plates and bound in a lone edition—his harsh invective proves much more durable. Dave inters his book one night in Michelle and Cal's garden, depositing it as a guide for his son, Carl. Instead of serving as paternal advice, however, it becomes the sacred text for the dystopian future. The men who discover and follow Dave's teachings use the book as the basis for the governing religious and political system of New London and Ingerland.

A revelatory text, the Book of Dave—distinguished from *The Book of Dave*—casts its author as an inverted version of St. John the Divine and the Koranic Mohammed. Not requiring a designated amanuensis or authorial surrogate, Dave speaks to an unintentional audience who then act as his philosophical conduits. At the end of his introduction to *Revelation*, Self writes of the final New Testament book that "this ancient text has survived to be the very stuff of modern, psychotic nightmare."[23] Ingerland is established in the wake of apocalyptic flooding, a deluge that transforms the landscape, but Dave's book, as its future followers come to understand it, "sets the parameters" as Self remarks of *Revelation*, which he considers a "sick text": "The riot of violent, imagistic occurrences; the cabalistic emphasis on numbers; the visceral repulsion expressed towards the bodily, the sensual and the sexual. It deranges in and of itself, and sets the parameters, marshals the props, for all the excessive playlets to come. In its vile obscuratinism is its baneful effect; the original language may have welded the metaphoric with the signified, the *logos* with the flesh, but in the King James version the text is a guignol of tedium, a portentous horror film."[24]

Here then lies the textual genesis of Dave's tirade. By taking the product of a rather ordinary fit of anger and depression, if not utter psychosis, and then transforming that text into a sacred document, Self slyly subverts the very notion of divine authority in such revered texts. Earthly and secular, in his moments of madness Dave is closer to the protagonist, Johnny, of Mike Leigh's 1993 film *Naked* than to the received images of ancient prophets.[25]

Dave Rudman's story is one of pain, desperation, and tragedy but also one of atonement and rebirth. He composes a redaction of his first book, which Carl and Cal Devenish place in a film canister and bury in their garden. As with the original book's internment as an ideologically explosive time capsule, this action has dramatic consequences for the future.

One of the most striking aspects of the novel is its argot, combining in various ways Received Pronunciation, Cockney and Mockney, a rural Essex dialect, Dave's private vocabulary and cab-drivers' slang, and the alpha-numerical substitutions of text messaging. Acting as both an aid to the reader for explaining the novel's idiolect and giving this language a heightened degree of authenticity, an "Arpee-English" glossary collates many of the novel's linguistic nuances and usages into an appendix. The novel's idiom—most especially the "mockni" of the Ingerland sections, which also uses diacritics to indicate inflections and visually resembles Celtic and Germanic languages—calls to mind similar phonetic mixtures in Anthony Burgess's Anglicized Russian vernacular, Nadsat, from *A Clockwork Orange* and the dialect in Russell Hoban's *Riddley Walker*. In his introduction to Alasdair Gray's novel *1982, Janine,* Self briefly discusses the structuralist relationships between fiction and reality, writing that the Scottish novelist's "word games are emphatically pre-modern. Rather than attempting to undermine the notion of objective truth by playing with the shattered fragments of the past, Gray shows us how our notions of reality are forced upon us by the relation in which they stand to one another."[26] Self's comments on the typographical and lexical qualities of Gray's novel encapsulate the overarching consequence of his own word-play in *The Book of Dave*. Whatever allusiveness Self might have intended, the overall effect remains essential to the novel. Just as the geography and customs that link the novel's two periods evolve and distort over time, language undergoes corresponding transformations to elicit poignancy and pathos as well as irony. Rather than a new Iron Age the residents of Ham, Chil, New London, and all of Ingerland exist in an Ironic Age, from the misprision stemming from the eponymous text to iron's renaming as "irony."

"Every generation gets the end-of-the-world anxiety it deserves," Self argues in his introduction to *Riddley Walker;* "it used to be transcendental, then it became elemental, and now it's environmental."[27] This sentiment holds true for *The Book of Dave*. Contemporary concerns such as environmentalism and animal rights figure prominently into Self's novel, though somewhat implicitly. As the denizens of Ham and other parts of rural Ingerland—even if such remote areas happen to occupy the same latitudinal and longitudinal coordinates as present-day

Hampstead—furtively gather and hoard physical relics that connect them spiritually to Dave's time, separating the authentic shards from the "toyist" ones, the reader quickly comprehends that in fact these characters are sorting through the refuse of the contemporary era. A culture of incessant disposability seems at odds with environmental health, but as Self illustrates it also can condition people into thinking of everything as a resource to be consumed, heedless of any ethical or moral considerations.

Motos figure prominently and poignantly in the chapters set in the distant future. Large, lisping, gentle creatures with porcine features, the motos allow for the Hamsters, as the inhabitants of secluded Ham are duly known, to indulge in the childish luxury of expressing compassion and love, to connect with their "mummy" (rather than "daddy") selves. The motos evolve in Self's fictional world from the emotos that appear in "Caring, Sharing" but have been conflated with automobiles or "motors." The motos appear as large children, seeking only the comforts of physical affection and wallowing in water, and they contrast with the utilitarian world of humans. Part of an initiation rite into manhood for the Hamsters is the sacrificial killing of the motos, followed by the rendering of their fat into the moto oil which provides the Hamsters with sustenance. The innocence and its destruction that the motos embody carry forward from Dave's time, a tragic realization of Dave's feelings for his son, Carl, whom as a toddler Dave thinks of as belonging to a hybrid species that exists to be loved and then sacrificed; indeed, the motos, as with the entirety of the Ingerland chapters, are the nightmarish projections of Dave's own fears and desire for retribution for not being allowed access to Carl. As with the names of the inhabitants, each of the moto names can be found in

Dave's era, all of them the nicknames of Carl's schoolmates—Runty, Boysie, Champ, and Tiger—revealing these two eras as conjoined in the dark recesses of Dave's psyche.

Important and minor characters from Self's previous works factor significantly into *The Book of Dave*. Gary "Fucker" Finch, whose pit bull meets its pathetic demise during one of Ian Wharton's most infamous outrages in *My Idea of Fun*, appears as one of Dave's closest friends, a fellow cabbie and a preposterous activist—and also pawn of Barry Higginbottom, the "Skip Tracer"—for father's rights as he garners publicity for his Fathers First support group. Busner makes a cameo in the novel, showing his famous Riddle and commenting on Shiva Mukti's unfortunate suicide, and Anthony Bohm appears in two guises in each of the two periods. While Busner and Bohm demonstrate a sense of narrative resiliency Jane Bowen has now become Jane Bernal, Dave's psychotherapist. Perhaps the most important recurring character in the novel, though, is Cal Devenish, who continues to act as an altar ego for Self's public persona. Having put drugs, commercial sex, and his career as a novelist behind him, Cal owns a successful television production company responsible for programs including *Bluey*, featuring a depressed dog that seems like a mixture of actual children's programs such as *Kipper* and *Blue's Clues*, further connecting the adult and children's worlds. Cal signifies on one level the public transformation that Self has undergone in his own career, renouncing a life of decadent excess for his family.

In many respects *The Book of Dave* appears as the culmination of much of Self's fictive interests. Themes that have doggedly shaped his novels, novellas, and short stories coalesce in this satiric novel in a finely-wrought way. Sexuality and gender identity, familial relationships and obligations, psychosis, and narrative ethics all play important parts in this work, overlapping and informing one another in significant ways. Self transforms the trappings of quotidian life into a mythopoeic narrative, an ambitious novel that yokes together the past, present, and future.

CHAPTER NINE

The Republic of Letters
Junk Mail, Sore Sites, Feeding Frenzy, and Other Nonfiction

"I write in Conrads" Self has explained of his writing habits. "Conrad wrote 800 words a day, on which he could support a butler, two maids, a chauffeur, a gardener and an under-gardener. On a good day, I write three Conrads, on a fighting day, four."[1] No one can doubt that Self has been a prolific writer; the debate centers more on the quality of the work than its quantity. When only a few years into his writing career, Self faced critical censure because of his highly productive work rate. His riposte to such critics revealed his self-confidence while appearing both defensive and aggressive: "It's not done, though, is it? To admit that you can sit down and write 30,000 words in 10 days. . . . If I was going to get arrogant, it'd be no problem. I could challenge any of those idiots to sit down in a glass booth and I could write the bollocks off them any day of the week. I am arrogant to that extent. I admit it shamelessly."[2] He certainly is not the only writer to produce a relatively large body of work in such a short time, but his is also a corpus of complexity, seriousness, and diversity. While his journalism and other excursions into the so-called republic of letters, that centuries-old figurative realm of political, cultural, and philosophical idea exchange, might at first seem like the "left-handed" activities of a writer biding his time between novels, these columns, reviews, and other occasional pieces constitute an important part of his writing career.

At various times Self has been the restaurant critic for the *Observer* (1995–97) and a columnist for the *Times* (1998–99), *Evening Standard,* and the *Independent.* He has published cultural criticism; book, film, and television reviews; and political commentary. In 2003 he began his "PsychoGeography" column for the *Independent,* free-ranging squibs about long-distance walking and other modes of travel, and the column continues his association with the illustrator Ralph Steadman, with whom he collaborated in 1987 for his election coverage for London's *New Statesman* magazine. Self also has written regular columns for *She,* the United States edition of *GQ,* and the architectural magazine *Building Design.* Although Self's three collections of nonfiction fairly represent much of the range of his nonfiction, and individual pieces occasionally restore editorial cuts, they cannot of course indicate the extent of these works. Further, Self frequently contributes introductions to other books, and these brief essays often illuminate his own works.

Split unevenly into two sections headed "On Drugs" and "On Other Things," Self's first nonfiction collection, *Junk Mail* (1995), resembles much of his life during this time. Although J. G. Ballard listed the book as one of his "Book of the Year" selections, calling it an "explosive collection,"[3] Will Eaves wrote in the *TLS* that its thematic division presents difficulties in reconciling Self's public personas. "Self the drug-crazed sybarite is not quite Self the prolific, hard-working novelist or columnist; he wants us to admire him in both guises, of course, but this we can only do if we accept that they are both part of the literary satirist's masquerade. It is a difficult balancing act."[4] Through *Junk Mail,* Self intersperses samples of his humorous line drawings, all done in the manner of his 1980s *New Statesman* comic strip, *Slump.*

Originally conceived during 1991 as "a book on drugs that would bring in some cash" when Self "was living outside Oxford and Broke," [5] *Junk Mail* retains this nascent thematic purpose in its title, early contents, and cover illustration of an envelope used for concealing and conveying narcotics. In the book's introduction Self reveals his unease about his original scheme for the volume. "I had been troubled by the idea of writing a book-length work exclusively on drugs for a number of reasons," he writes. "First and foremost there was my very English dread of, as De Quincey put it, 'twitching away the decent drapery' and revealing personal scars and chancres to the eyes of the world. I knew damn well that a large part of what sold the treatment of the book to its potential publisher was the expectation that I would publicly grass on myself" (ix–x). Instead of confession, however, Self offers social examination. In the first section, which takes up less than a third of the volume, Self discusses all aspects of drugs from street-dealing to recovery programs, and he includes reviews of various books dealing in some fashion with drugs and society, with special attention given to William Burroughs. What seems most significant about these pieces, though, is neither Self's extensive knowledge of the lifestyles involving drug use nor his proselytizing about drug legislation but the intercessions this plays in his fiction. "New Crack City," a 1991 *Evening Standard* article, anticipates the milieu of his London noir trilogy while "Let Us Intoxicate" deals with one aspect of social rituals, a key underpinning of his fiction and fictional world.

The remaining larger section of the collection continues to demonstrate the various ways that Self's journalism can inform his fiction. He brings together discussions of motorways; reviews of seminal influences such as Woody Allen, Louis-Ferdinand Céline, and Joseph Heller; and interviews with Martin Amis and

J. G. Ballard. Elements of each of these subjects appear in Self's fiction. Similarly, "Dealing with the Devil" looks back to *My Idea of Fun* while "Head-hunting for Eternity," a feature article on Cyroniscists in California, provides him part of his material for the Los Angeles section of *Dorian* much in the way that "On the Edge of Blackness" relates to the Australian section of *How the Dead Live*. Self continues to show the symbiotic nature between his journalism and fiction, including basing the rabbit-hunting scene near the end of *The Book of Dave* on a 2005 "PsychoGeography" column.[6] Such carrying over is no mere recycling of material but instead a demonstration of the ways that certain ideas cross easily between Self's actual and alternative worlds.

At one point in the volume's introduction, Self admits that much of the book "represents the fruits of being prepared to do more or less what my editor asks me to do, having calculated the ratio of glibness to money that the commission represents" (xi). Such is the nature of writing for hire, even in literary journalism. As he continues, though, Self expresses his dissatisfaction at ephemeral samples of his journalism gaining attention while the public takes little notice of more contemplative articles. One example of this discrepancy, he points out, is with "The Valley of the Corn Dollies," which he "agonised over for a full month, and which then was published to resounding silence on all fronts" (xi). The most impressive piece in the volume, this cultural essay is a meditation on English identity. In addition to deconstructing much of contemporary English culture, Self also associates his brand of satire as a native tradition, claiming that "England has the world's top satirical culture" and that "the English have, in the two and a half centuries since Swift . . . ascended a parabola of facetiousness to achieve the very zenith of irony. We have managed this by fostering a culture of conflict and opposition" (204). Although Self at one point in the essay errs by attributing authorship of Richard Eyre's 1984 polemical film *The Ploughman's Lunch* to David Hare rather than to Ian McEwan (214), the piece remains a shrewd assessment of English culture during the late twentieth century.

Whereas *Junk Mail* culled its selections from a variety of publications, Self's second collection of nonfiction, *Sore Sites* (2000), brings together samples taken solely from his weekly column for *Building Design*. Unlike *Junk Mail* and *Feeding Frenzy* this collection contains no introduction, only a one-sentence prefatory note, though like its predecessor it contains several of Self's illustrations. The volume reads like the transcript of an ongoing monologue as Self holds sway on a variety of topics connected, loosely at times, to architecture. Precursors of his "PsychoGeography" columns, these selections show Self wandering around London and other regions of England, commenting on the aesthetics of buildings; although in some of the columns he never leaves home, literally or figuratively, discussing aspects of domestic life at *chez* Self. The presiding tones of these pieces are irony and humor: even when making serious points about Self's preoccupations (narrative and otherwise) they impart a self-deprecating conviviality.

In "Not to Scale," Self briefly discusses the relationship between his surrealist mode of fiction and "the conundrum that the very notion of scale presents us with—time and time again." After a paragraph-long discourse on the "different complexes or gestalts bound up in the notion of scale," he counters this with his wife's suggestion that this preoccupation results from his height: "While, at 6 foot 5 inches, I fall an inch short of official giganticism, I have nonetheless spent a lot of my adult life head-butting the architrave."[7] This leads him to a discussion of Lancing College, founded by Self's great-great-grandfather Nathaniel Woodard. Because the chapel of this school stands disproportionately to the rest of Lancing College, with a "nave bigger than Notre Dame's," Self sums up his ancestor as a "grandiose nutter" (57–58). Throughout this collection, Self mixes such humorous asides with descriptions of other preoccupations and biographical details that pop up in various ways in his fiction.

Occasionally in his fiction, most noticeably in *The Book of Dave,* Self takes care to distinguish London brick from any other type. In "Stock Brickies," Self describes his jobs as a laborer, first as a nineteen-year-old hod-carrier and then for eight months after leaving Oxford as a "driver-cum-labourer for a general builders' firm" (26). Essentially a tribute to the skills of builders and laborers this article also gives Self the opportunity to engage in public self-examination. Although he only worked as a laborer for some eight months, Self writes that "I learnt to tell a putlock from an Acrow prop, and a London from a stock brick. I learnt the location of the vast, secret hinterland of builders' merchants that exists in every city—but most importantly I learnt how to labour" (26). When Self draws upon such knowledge in his fiction his work gains an air of authority and verisimilitude as well as imagistic precision. While Self's vocation in construction was short-lived, in these columns he touches upon areas of significance to his brother and father; Self's father was an expert in city planning and his half-brother, Nicholas Adams, is a professor of architectural history. These columns bring together all of these elements, explicitly and implicitly, and point out the psychic connections that one can have to buildings and locations —the "psychogeography" that figures so prominently in much of his writing elsewhere. The volume contains several accounts of growing up in north London's Hampstead Garden Suburb, and in the concluding piece, "Phobiaground," Self writes what entails part of the poignancy in his short story "The Five-swing Walk." "Playgrounds—even the more 'adventurous' kind—are really phobiagrounds, in which children learn to fear the world they live in, and accept a future in which they will live in 'gated' communities, protected from the rest of society by armed security guards" (237).

Self devotes several columns to his childhood in the section of north London where he grew up, divulging details that have appeared in *How the Dead Live* and other works. In "The Weins Will Hear You," he discusses his neighbors: a widow named Mrs. Rubens on one side, and a couple named Lewis and Mary Wein, founders of a dry-goods wholesale business called Lew-Mar (104–5). These couples provide the model for Lewis and Mary Rubens, owners of the same business in *How the Dead Live*. The significance of these articles lies not merely in their ability to provide factual glosses for his fiction but to reveal the importance that the north London suburbs had and continues to have on Self. As he writes in one article, "I was poised between the devil and the deep blue sea, because at around 12, when I was forced to abandon my RP in favour of Mockney I had to say that I lived in East Finchley, the very acme of dull outer-London suburbs" (95). Yet as he concludes "The Weins Will Hear you," Self remarks that physical and temporal separation, along with fatherhood, has given him a new perspective on this area. "I hated suburbia and got out as quickly as I could, but driving out there from the inner city, what struck me first is what strikes everybody else: the space, the lack of on-road parking, the greenery . . . I feel a reversion to type coming over me" (106). It is unsurprising that Self would revisit these suburbs again in his fiction, particularly in *The Book of Dave*.

Four years after the *Observer* fired him, Self published *Feeding Frenzy,* which looks back at this time of shambles through its very title. In his introduction to the collection Self addresses this well-publicized event and strives to set forth the facts, writing that "what remains pertinent is that I myself then became the human bait for a media feeding frenzy."[8] Deborah Orr, Self's wife and a journalist well regarded for her columns and editorial acumen, "characterised this at the time as an example of a new kind of story in the British press, 'the broadsheet tabloid story.' This she defined as a story that should have been of interest only to tabloid readers, but was blown out of all proportion by broadsheet journalists behaving like gutter hacks" (vi–vii). The title of this collection embraces more than his 1997 imbroglio; it suggests both his "propensity for writing/feeding too much" and his tenure as a restaurant critic for the *Observer* (v). A collection of 129 reviews, articles, radio essays, and other assorted occasional pieces, *Feeding Frenzy* covers the period 1995–2001, picking up where *Junk Mail* ended.

Because the volume dispenses with titles and follows neither chronological nor a clearly thematic organization, its index serves multiple purposes as a quick-reference guide and a catalogue that "covers not only people, places and things, but also ideas, obsessions and my own irritating stylistic tics" (ix). These tics include sending the reader on something of a whimsical walkabout through the index as Self directs to them multiple entries. Despite what first seems like a random ordering of the articles, they begin to acquire continuity. Self's restaurant reviews typify his streak of impish satire, deflating the pomposity of 1990s-era haute cuisine. Self has famously irked many chefs and restaurant owners—not for giving their food a bad review but for ignoring it all together, a calculated assault on their egos. At other times he devoted his review to chain restaurants such as Pizza Express, and for his final column Self compared two restaurants: a McDonald's branch and the venerable Michelin-three-star-rated La Tante Claire, where the final bills amounted to £4.97 and £194.20 respectively (366). In these reviews and in his "Self Critical" column for the *Times,* Self invents fictional companions such as "Dave the Power Ranger and Dave the Garagiste" (253), Dr. Klangenfarben, and Dr. "Big" McFee of the Glasgow Royal Infirmary, his "quondam neurologist" (33), and even recounts trips to the fictional Sealink Club which figures so importantly into the Soho of his alternate fictional universe. As one reviewer observes, "The influence gonzo reportage has had on Self's writing is clear. And it's what is most impressive: Self often writes non-fiction as though it were fiction, topping off what we know as reality with the cream of his surreality."[9]

Self's article on Hunter S. Thompson begins by attempting to capture the essence of Thompson's *Fear and Loathing in Las Vegas* before discussing the influence this work had on Self as a teenager. Noting Thompson's broader influence on journalists, Self remarks that "even the most asinine and self-regarding 'columnist' may employ gonzo techniques in the process of baring his or her emotional breast in public. It is far more acceptable now to pass satire off as reality—even if both are banal. Perhaps this is the counterpart—in terms of reportage—to J. G. Ballard's observation that the job of fiction writers has become to invent reality, because reality itself is so fictive" (371). This article, which appeared in the *New Statesman* just before the brouhaha concerning Self's activities on John Major's campaign jet,[10] ends on an ironically prescient note: "I just don't see too many journalists around at the moment who are prepared to get themselves into a state where they see their dead grand-mother crawling up their leg with a knife in her teeth, and—damn it all!—still file" (372). Although this sentiment conveys unintentional irony in the light of the election debacle, and is sub-sequently notable for the way in which it relates to the impli-cations of the volume's title, as a whole *Feeding Frenzy* is more significant for its measuring of Self's journalism career from 1995 to 2001, making it a complementary companion to *Junk Mail*.

Just as *Junk Mail* reaches its finest point with "Valley of the Corn Dollies," *Feeding Frenzy* achieves a similar moment in the essay Self wrote for *Granta*, "Big Dome." In this article—unti-tled in *Feeding Frenzy*, in keeping with all other pieces the collection assembles—Self hits upon a masterstroke of psycho-geography, describing at length the psychic effects that London has long had on him. It is, he writes, a vast metropolis "filled in with narratives, which have been extruded like psychic mastic into its fissures. . . . To traverse central London today, even in a car, even on autopilot, is still to run over a hundred memories" (37). Self discusses incorporating the city as a vital part of his fic-tion from "Waiting" and other stories in *The Quantity Theory of Insanity* to *Great Apes*, reinforcing the intimate connections his fictional world has with its actual counterpart. The surreal-ism of Self's fiction, in fact, owes much to the way that London appears as a jumble of paradoxes, a mélange of apparent antithe-ses which don't so much quarrel with one another as insist that the reader comprehend them all simultaneously. "There's only way to arrest the entropy of the city—keep writing about it," Self proclaims. "I've learned to accept London as my muse. Initially, there I was, sitting on the tube, when she came in: filthy, raddled, smelly, old and drunk. Like everyone else I wanted to get up and move to the next carriage, especially when she elected to sit down right next to me. But now we're inseparable, going round and round the Circle Line, arm in arm, perhaps for eternity" (43).

Self's nonfiction is not limited to journalism. While *Feeding Frenzy* reprints catalogue copy from Sebastian Horsley and Sam Taylor-Wood art exhibitions, these pieces are odd short stories that question their very form. Self has produced similar pieces, of significantly varying length, for the artists Marc Quinn, Nicola Hicks, and others, while also contributing to books featuring the work of David Shrigley and Antony Gormley among others. Self has written frequently about contemporary art, approvingly and negatively, and has written a profile of Jo Self, a respected artist and former wife of Self's brother Jonathan, for *Modern Painters*. An early advocate of Damien Hirst, whom he interviewed for *Modern Painters*, Self has also been highly critical of much of the London-based art milieu. Commenting on the 1996 Turner Prize finalists, lately a guaranteed source of mild controversy, Self objects that "the most obvious meanings embedded in all four artists' efforts are meta-meanings, meanings that arrive somewhere between the contemplation of the object itself and the contemplation of the catalogue copy that grounds it in explanation."[11]

A key part of Self's uncollected work is the body of work that introduces other writers' and artists' work. Indeed, a modest yet diverse collection can be culled simply from his original contributions to other books. He has provided introductory essays to volumes by Georges Bataille, William Burroughs, Lewis Carroll,

Russell Hoban, and several others. In his foreword to a collection of essays on postmodernism Self succinctly lays open one problem of postmodern critical theory, illustrating an application of Jean Baudrillard's conception of simulacra: "It's a sad fact about the landscape of postmodernism that so much is a mirage of a mirage, a complex set of interactions between convection (hot air) and reflection (unoriginality) resulting in the superimposition of one illusion upon another."[12] When Self writes favorably, though no less critically, on a subject his prose conveys his enthusiasm in its rhythms and scope.

His introduction to a reissue of Alasdair Gray's *1982, Janine*, for example, celebrates the novel and its author alike, but it also addresses questions regarding narrative complexity relevant to all of literature: "Why should we trouble ourselves with difficult books? Why should we not slurp fictional mush and be spoon-fed undemanding narratives? For the simple reason that if literature doesn't have a capacity for awkwardness, then it cannot convey anything of the unreality of what it is like to be in this world."[13] Such platforms allow Self to voice his philosophy on the roles that art (and literature) and the artist undertake, and while at times he buttresses his own narrative idiosyncrasies and approach he also engages in a serious exchange of ideas.

This is not to say that all of Self's published work is serious. Many pieces, in fact, have a strong tone of frivolity while others appear as little more than verbal exercises, extended jokes, self-promotion, or contractual fulfillments, and give credence to Self's own description of his position as a hack if not, as in *The Sweet Smell of Psychosis*, a superhack. The overwhelming majority, though, express sincere ideas and opinions, some of which have evolved or shifted during the course of his career. Although some commentators have complained of his media ubiquity and prodigious productivity, in essence he is a throw-back to an earlier era where writers engaged in all realms of cultural discourse. In carrying forward the traditions of previous essayists and satirists, he challenges contemporary notions of literary balkanization.

Self's nonfiction cannot be entirely disentangled from his fiction. At times he uses devices and techniques more freely available to the novelist than to the journalist, including fictional characters. His "Self Critical" column for London's *Times* newspaper, to take only one example, contains a recurring character: Dr. John "Big" McFee of the Glasgow Royal Infirmary, who purportedly functions as the author's neurologist and social companion as well as his narrative foil. A Scottish counterpart of sorts to Dr. Zack Busner, McFee becomes an insistent resident of Self's fictional alternate society. "Just you try lasting a few days without my healing influence," he claims to Self in one column; "then we'll see what a sick bunnykins you become."[14] At other times, Self's essays and reviews provide insight into his creative processes.

His review of *The Complete Prose of Woody Allen*, "Not a Great Decade to Be Jewish," reveals not only Self's particular identification with his Jewish-American ancestry—"the touchstone of whatever Semitism I accorded myself"[15]—but also the affinity Allen's comic gags affords him and how Self has integrated Allen's mode of humor into his own comedy and satire. Self declares this influence through imitation and allusion. Whereas in his review Self observes that "his use of pastiche and parody . . . represent the seedbed of Allen's humorous vision,"[16] in "The Quantity Theory of Insanity" Self establishes one aspect of his own humor through his parody and pastiche of academic prose. The basic structures and rhythms of Allen's comic prose reverberate throughout Self's fiction, particularly his deadpan jokes. After identifying Allen's "comic one-liners" as "a painful of involution of the existential aphorism" and acts of unabashedly intellectual display, Self speculates that perhaps his "discomfort on rereading these pieces was as much a function of recognizing this pretension within myself as of seeing it in Allen."[17] Certainly the casual repudiation of supernatural events at the center of "The North London Book of the Dead" entails one example of this tendency: "When you die you move to another part of London, that's all there is to it. Period."[18] Allen's "Notes from the Overfed," in which a grotesquely obese man whose flesh drips off him "like hot fudge from a sundae"[19] and who supplies a discourse on the physics and metaphysics of human fat, has an important presence in *My Idea of Fun* and *How the Dead Live*. At one point Allen's narrator asks, "Could not all life be an illusion? Indeed, are there not certain sects of holy men in the East who are convinced that *nothing* exists outside their minds except for the Oyster Bar at Grand Central Station?"[20] This passage provides Self's first novel with the title and setting of its epilogue ("At The Oyster Bar of Grand Central Station"), and it gives his third novel key images regarding the book's main conceit, Lily Bloom and the Fats that haunt her Dulston flat. In *How the Dead Live* Self extends Allen's ice cream simile, transforming it into the novel's multiple references to ice cream. There are moments in "Not a Great Decade to be Jewish" when Self could be discussing his own work. Observing Allen's intertextual play in pieces such as "The Kugelmass Episode," which uses the conceit of projecting Allen's antiheroic protagonist into Gustave Flaubert's novel *Madame Bovary*, Self avers that this method creates "a *reductio ad absurdum* of fantasy/reality, reality/fantasy, that is the hallmark of true satire."[21]

This perpetually reflecting combination of the actual and imagined, of reality and fantasy, furnishes the foundations of Self's alternative fictional universe and his various means of inviting his readers into it.

Only by imagining the various genres in which Self writes as, perhaps, particular districts in his alternative universe can readers fully appreciate the ways in which they intersect. Despite the amount of time he has given to writing journalism, and the voluminous body of prose he has penned for hire, Self regards his nonfiction as secondary to his novels and short stories. "Fiction is where I really find myself as a writer," he once told the journalist Lynn Barber. "It's the mother lode. It's where I get my jollies."[22] For all its frequent irony and intellectual exhibitions, Self's nonfiction remains, like his fiction, rooted in the pleasures of the imagination.

Notes

Chapter 1: Understanding Will Self

1. See Nicholas Lezard, "Naughty Bits of a Shaggy Dog," *Independent* (London), 1 Nov. 1992, 33; Jason Cowley, "Habit Forming," *Times* (London), 24 June 2000, 14; Sarah Lyall, "Tale of Recovery from a Bad Boy of Letters," *New York Times,* 16 Oct. 2000, E1; Zulfikar Abbany, "Self-Service," review of *Feeding Frenzy, Observer* (London), 11 Nov. 2001, 17.

2. Zoë Heller, "Self Examination," *Vanity Fair,* June 1993, 126.

3. Salman Rushdie, "20–20 Vision," *Independent on Sunday* (London), 17 Jan. 1993, Sunday Review section, 24.

4. Self's episode of the BBC's *Correspondent* program, "Addicted to Arms: A Will Self Investigation," was broadcast on 28 April 2002.

5. Will Self, "Will Self," in *The Cost of Letters,* ed. Andrew Holgate and Honor Wilson-Fletcher (London: Waterstone's, 1998), 127.

6. Lynn Barber, "Self Control," *Observer* (London), 11 June 2000, Life section, 17.

7. John Walsh, "Bully Puts His Soul up for Sale," *Independent* (London), 18 Sept. 1993, 28.

8. Tom Shone, "Slimes of Suburbia," *Observer* (London), 22 Dec. 1991, 42.

9. John Keenan, "Private Dysfunctions," *Sunday Times* (London), 27 Nov. 1994, 15.

10. Will Self, *Junk Mail* (London: Bloomsbury, 1995), 401.

11. Will Self, introduction to *Alice's Adventures in Wonderland,* by Lewis Carroll (London and New York: Bloomsbury, 2001), xii–xiii.

12. Will Self, "Will Self" in *Un véritable naturalisme littéraire est-il possible ou même souhaitable?* (Nantes: Éditions Plains Feux, 2003), 44–46.

13. Stephen Smith, "In the Psychiatrist's Chair Is a Very Dangerous Place to Be," review of *Dr Mukti, Observer* (London), 18 Jan. 2004, 17.

14. Will Self, in an interview on the Penguin (UK) author page, http://www.penguin.co.uk.

15. Heller, "Self Examination," 148.

16. Will Self, "Clearing My Mind over Mater," *Times* (London), 22 Oct. 1992, 19.

17. Will Self and David Gamble, *Perfidious Man* (London: Viking, 2000), 4–5.

18. Will Self, "Big Dome," *Granta 65* (Spring 1999), 118.

19. Jonathan Self, *Self Abuse* (London: John Murray, 2001), 38.

20. Penny Drinkwater and Elaine Self, *A Passion for Garlic* (London: Duckworth, 1980).

21. J. Self, *Self Abuse,* 18–19.

22. Ibid., 19.

23. Self and Gamble, *Perfidious Man,* 4.

24. J. Self, *Self Abuse,* 26.

25. Ibid., 26–27.

26. Will Self, *The Quantity Theory of Insanity* (London: Bloomsbury, 1991), 4.

27. Tom Shone, "The Complete, Unexpurgated Self," *Sunday Times Magazine* (London), 5 Sept. 1993, 41.

28. John Springs, "Self Examination," *Independent* (London), 3 May 1997, Features section, 7.

29. J. Self, *Self Abuse,* 87.

30. Self and Gamble, *Perfidious Man,* 5.

31. Will Self, *My Idea of Fun: A Cautionary Tale* (London: Bloomsbury, 1993), 25.

32. Nick Rennison, *Contemporary British Novelists* (London: Routledge, 2005), 150.

33. Shone, "Complete, Unexpurgated Self," 39.

34. Self, *Junk Mail,* 59.

35. J. Self, *Self Abuse,* 161.

36. "Bull" appears in *Cock & Bull: Twin Novellas* (London: Bloomsbury, 1992) and "The Indian Mutiny" in *Grey Area and Other Stories* (London: Bloomsbury, 1994).

37. Springs, "Self Examination," 28.

38. Shone, "Complete, Unexpurgated Self," 41.

39. Ibid.

40. Ibid.

41. Will Self, *Slump, New Statesman,* 27 June 1985, 14.

42. J. G. Ballard, "The Innocent as Paranoid," in *The User's Guide to the Millennium* (London: HarperCollins, 1996), 91–98. See also J. G. Ballard, introduction to *Crash* (New York: Vintage, 1985), 1.

43. Will Self, *Dorian: An Imitation* (London: Viking/Penguin, 2002), 59.

44. Laurie Taylor, "The Luxury of Doubt," *New Humanist,* Sept. 2003, 14.

45. Self, "Will Self," in *Un véritable naturalisme littéraire,* 48, 50.

46. Heller, "Self Examination," 151.

Chapter 2: Urban Bedlam

1. The British hardcover edition, published in 1993, was included in the Bloomsbury Classics series. Its inclusion as a "classic" two years after its original publication suggests both the publisher's optimism for the book and a strategy for marketing Self between the publication of *Cock & Bull* and *My Idea of Fun.* According to Self, the book's publication in the United States was postponed due to a lack of name recognition at the time and "the classic canard about being able to flog short stories" (Anna Henchman, "Will Self: An Enfant Terrible Comes of Age," *Publishers Weekly,* 8 Sept. 1997, 53).

2. "Books for Christmas," *Independent,* 1 Dec. 1991, 28.

3. Self, *The Quantity Theory of Insanity,* 1. Parenthetical references are to the Bloomsbury edition. However, as with nearly all of Self's titles the subsequent U.S. editions (New York: Grove/Atlantic,

1994; New York: Vintage, 1995) duplicate the original pagination and typesetting.

4. Self, *Junk Mail,* 390.

5. Ibid., 391.

6. Philip Tew, *The Contemporary British Novel* (London: Continuum, 2004), 99.

7. Peter Self, *Cities in Flood* (London: Faber and Faber, 1957), 20.

8. Nick Hornby, "Mad about Insanity," *Times Literary Supplement,* 20 Dec. 1991, 25.

9. Thomas Mallon, *In Fact: Essays on Writers and Writing* (New York: Pantheon, 2001), 97.

10. In "Inclusion®" Simon Dykes—who is nominally linked to Simon Gurney—likewise calls Busner "the Hierophant," reinforcing the continuity of Busner's history, and he further remarks of Busner that "the way he surreptitiously tinkered with the architecture of my mind is an obscenity." Self, *Grey Area,* 245.

11. See Shone, "Complete, Unexpurgated Self," 41.

12. "You Ask the Questions: Will Self," *Independent,* 6 June 2001, Features section, 7.

13. Steven Connor, *The English Novel in History 1950–1995* (London: Routledge, 1996), 70.

14. Liorah Anne Golomb, "The Fiction of Will Self: Motif, Method and Madness," in *Contemporary British Fiction,* ed. Richard J. Lane, Rod Mengham, and Philip Tew (Cambridge: Polity Press, 2003), 80.

Chapter 3: Hermaphrodites and Hermeneutics

1. Self, *Junk Mail,* 381.

2. Self, *Cock & Bull,* 44. Parenthetical references are to the Bloomsbury edition.

3. Natasha Walter, "Congenital Failings," *Times Literary Supplement,* 9 Oct. 1992, 22.

4. Anthony Quinn, "Nouvelle Vague," *London Review of Books,* 7 Jan. 1993, 20.

5. Janet Harbord, "Performing Parts: Gender and Sexuality in Recent Fiction and Theory," *Women: A Cultural Review* 7, no. 1 (1996):42.

6. Ibid., 44.

7. Self, *Junk Mail,* 394.

8. Self and Gamble, *Perfidious Man,* 7.

9. Ibid., 7–8.

10. In the epigraph, Self mistakenly replaces "heath" at the end of the second line with "edges," a confusion caused perhaps by the "red ribb'd ledges" in line three of "Maud."

11. Important discussions of these competing methods appear in, among other sources, David Lodge, *The Novelist at the Crossroads* (Ithaca: Cornell University Press, 1971); Iris Murdoch's polemic essay "Against Dryness" in Malcolm Bradbury's *The Novel Today* (London: Fontana, 1977); and Robert Scholes, *The Fabulators* (New York: Oxford University Press, 1967).

12. Craig Seligman, "Buster Keaton in Hell," *New Yorker,* 11 Apr. 1994, 89.

13. Tom Shone, "Body Language," *Sunday Times* (London), 1 Nov. 1992, Books section, 12.

14. Self, *Junk Mail,* 341.

15. Shone, "Complete, Unexpurgated Self," 42.

Chapter 4: Empathy for the Devil

1. Heller, "Self Examination," 127.

2. Self, *Junk Mail,* 221.

3. Elizabeth Young, "Rough Magic," *New Statesman,* 10 Sept. 1993, 38.

4. Taylor, "The Luxury of Doubt," 12.

5. Self, *My Idea of Fun,* 11. Parenthetical references are to the Bloomsbury edition; however, subsequent editions in the United Kingdom and the United States contain identical pagination.

6. See "Will Self Climbs aboard Thomas the Tank Engine," *Guardian* (London), 22 Nov. 2003, Weekend Review section, 4. Referring to Sodor as a "prelapsarian Eden," Self briefly discusses

the influence of the *Thomas the Tank Engine* series on *My Idea of Fun:* "If only we'd all listened to the Fat Controller and done what he told us to do, none of the ensuing mess would've occurred! I was so taken by The Fat Controller (or rather, by the all-powerfully politically incorrect essence of the fellow), that I named a sinister character in my first novel after him. A very sinister character. My Fat Controller did truly unspeakable things, directing the lives of mere mortals as if they were animate engines, forced to run on preordained tracks." Self has also written about Awdry's series in his "Psycho-Geography" column: see "PsychoGeography #61: The Truth about Thomas the Tank Engine," *Independent* (London), 27 Nov. 2004, 9.

7. Will Self, "PsychoGeography #96: It's Stranger on a Train," *Independent* (London), 6 Aug. 2005, Features section, 7.

8. Friedrich Nietzsche, *Beyond Good and Evil,* trans. Walter Kaufmann (New York: Vintage, 1989), 203.

8. Colin MacCabe, "Reluctant Psychopath," *London Review of Books,* 7 Oct. 1993, 20.

9. Heller, "Self Examination," 151.

10. Shone, "Complete, Unexpurgated Self," 42.

11. Anthony Quinn, "Hammering the Horror," *Sunday Times* (London), 12 Sept. 1993, Section 6, 12.

12. Phil Baker, "Tutorials from Hell," *Times Literary Supplement,* 10 Sept. 1993, 22.

13. Julian Evans, "A Severed Neck," *Guardian* (London), 14 Sept. 1993, 12.

14. The Brighton scenes in the novel suggest personal significance for Self. His father's family had been prominent residents of Brighton, and as a child Self visited his grandparents there frequently. Jonathan Self discusses this in his memoir, *Self Abuse.*

15. Will Self, "World of Serial," *Big Issue,* 31 May 1994, 33.

16. Self, *Junk Mail,* 367.

Chapter 5: The Death of Affect

1. Peter Kemp, "Private Dysfunction," *Sunday Times* (London), 27 Nov. 1994, 15.

2. Will Eaves, "Beaconsfield Philosophers," *Times Literary Supplement,* 18 Nov. 1994, 20.

3. James Saynor, "Through the Eye of a Needle," *Observer* (London), 2 Nov. 1994, 19.

4. Mallon, *In Fact,* 97.

5. Ballard, introduction to *Crash,* 1. See also Ballard, "The Innocent as Paranoid," 91–98.

6. Self, *My Idea of Fun,* 229.

7. Self, *Grey Area,* 16. Parenthetical references are to the Bloomsbury edition.

8. Self's narrator bears a faint psychological resemblance to the delusional school master dying from radiation poisoning who narrates Martin Amis's short story "The Immortals" in *Einstein's Monsters* (London: Jonathan Cape, 1987; New York: Harmony, 1987), a character that likewise attempts to replace his quotidian existence with a self-imposed fantasy of power and extraordinary privileges.

9. John Crace, "Self Made Man," *Guardian* (London), 27 June 2000, Education section, 6.

10. Stein appears previously in Self's fiction as the millenarian philosopher Richard Stein who gives a lecture in "Waiting."

11. Jonathan Coe, *What a Carve Up!* (Harmondsworth: Penguin, 1994). The American edition was retitled *The Winshaw Legacy* (New York: Knopf, 1995).

12. Self, *Junk Mail,* 59.

13. Will Self, *Feeding Frenzy* (London: Viking, 2001), 41.

14. *Granta* 43 (Spring 1993), 257–73.

15. Bomb the Bass, *Clear* (Island Records, 1995).

16. Eaves, "Beaconsfield Philosophers," 20.

17. Self, *Junk Mail,* 131.

18. This story's subtitle, "The Impossibility of Self-Determination as to Desire," appears to satirize the pretensions of the titles of works by controversial British artist Damien Hirst. One of his most infamous works, a 1991 installation featuring a tiger shark suspended in a tank of formaldehyde, is entitled *The Physical Impossibility of Death in the Mind of Someone Living.*

Chapter 6: London Noir

1. Will Self, *The Sweet Smell of Psychosis* (London: Bloomsbury, 1996), 11. Parenthetical references are to this edition.

2. Self, *Feeding Frenzy*, 129.

3. Ibid.

4. As with *Get Out!,* for which John Bull works in *Bull, Rendezvous* appears to be loosely modeled on *Time Out*. Strengthening this connection between his second and third novellas Self has Richard "annotating pre-puff for Razza Rob's new stand-up show *Gynae-Gynae, Hey-Hey!*" (41), a reference to the stand-up comic who possibly triggers Bull's genital transmutation.

5. Headed by Toby Young and Julie Burchill, the *Modern Review* actively promoted Self early in his career and also had on its staff Cosmo Landesman and Tom Shone, both of whom have written about Self for other publications.

6. For the Limehouse scene, see *Dorian*, chapter 16. Danny O'Toole makes a cameo appearance on page 218 of the novel.

7. Self, *Junk Mail*, 208–9.

8. Ibid., 11.

9. Ibid.

10. Will Self, *Tough, Tough Toys for Tough, Tough Boys* (London: Bloomsbury, 1998), 3. Parenthetical references are to this edition.

11. For further details concerning the thematic links between the London noir trilogy, or "triella," and F. Scott Fitzgerald, see Brian Finney, "The Sweet Smell of Excess: Will Self, Bataille and Transgression," http://www.csulb.edu/~bhfinney/WillSelf.html. Finney's essay contains insightful readings of several important themes in Self's fiction.

12. Self, *Junk Mail*, 15.

13. "Joseph Andrews" is also the name of a crime boss in Martin Amis's short story "State of England" (1996) and novel *Yellow Dog* (2003), a work in which the significance of the name features prominently.

14. Self, *The Quantity Theory of Insanity,* 114.

15. Barber, "Self Control," 14.

Chapter 7: Souls in Conflict

1. Chris Blackhurst, "Self: Why I Did It, Why I Lied," *The Independent on Sunday* (London), 20 Apr. 1997, 3.

2. Will Self, *Great Apes* (London: Bloomsbury, 1997), 1. Parenthetical references are to this edition.

3. Self, *Feeding Frenzy,* 136.

4. John Gray, *Straw Dogs: Thoughts on Humans and Other Animals* (London: Granta, 2002), 24.

5. Ibid., 38.

6. Self, *Feeding Frenzy,* 138.

7. Cole Moreton, "Simian Says," *Independent* (London), 8 June 1997, 29.

8. Ra Page, "Monkey Puzzles," *Guardian* (London), 1 May 1997, T15.

9. Self, *Grey Area,* 247.

10. Ballard, introduction to *Crash,* 3.

11. Will Self, "Ingenious Bubble Wrap," *New Statesman,* 15 July 2002, 48.

12. Taylor, "The Luxury of Doubt," 14–15.

13. Elaine Showalter, "Posthumous Parenting," *Guardian* (London), 17 June 2000, 9.

14. Tom Shone, "Something to Offend Everyone," *New York Times Book Review,* 8 Oct. 2000, 8.

15. Will Self, interview by James Naughtie, *Bookclub,* BBC Radio 4, 3 Oct. 2004.

16. Self, *Junk Mail,* 287, 290. The Whitechapel branch of Blooms appears in an early chapter of *The Book of Dave.*

17. Will Self, "Why I Hate Easter," *Independent* (London), 2 Apr. 1999, Features section, 1. More recently in his newspaper columns Self has written of his newfound admiration for Christmas. See "Why I'm Fool for Yule," *Evening Standard* (London), 23 Dec.

2005, 13; "PsychoGeography #115: The Plot against Santa," *Independent* (London), 31 Dec. 2005, Features section, 7.

18. Self, "Why I Hate Easter," 1.

19. Rude Boy shares a name with his father, Dave Kaplan, Lily's first husband, and also with David Yaws, her second husband. This use of the name "Dave," which Self utilizes as a sort of contemporary Everyman identity, suggests among other things the universal themes of the novel.

20. Will Self, *How the Dead Live* (London: Bloomsbury, 2000), 151. Parenthetical references are to this edition.

21. Self, *Feeding Frenzy,* 286.

22. For a discussion of the actual LewMar see "The Weins Will Hear You," *Sore Sites* (London: Ellipsis, 2000), 104–6; reprinted with restored editorial cuts in *Feeding Frenzy,* 223–25. As this article reveals, Lewis and Mary Rubens are a composite of two sets of Self's neighbors during his childhood in north London, the Weins and a widow named Mrs. Rubens.

23. The birth years of David Jr. and Charlotte also conform to those of Self's brothers, Nick Adams and Jonathan Self.

24. Taylor, "The Luxury of Doubt," 12.

Chapter 8: "Here and There, Now and Then"

1. Self, *Dorian,* 267. Parenthetical references are to the Viking edition.

2. Self, *Feeding Frenzy,* 377. This article first appeared in the February 2000 issue of *GQ* (U.S.).

3. Self, "Ingenious Bubble Wrap," 49.

4. Will Self, "It's a Wild, Wilde World," *Guardian* (London), 5 July 2003, 31.

5. Robert McCrum, "Self Analysis," interview, *Observer Review* (London), 29 Sept. 2002, 15.

6. Neil Bartlett, "Picture of Ill-Health," *Guardian* (London), 21 Sept. 2002, 26.

7. Ibid.

8. McCrum, "Self Analysis," 15.

9. Will Self, "Identity Crisis," *Independent Review* (London), 27 Sept. 2002, 5.

10. Ibid.

11. Ibid., 4.

12. Richard Canning, "Outdoing Wilde in Sex, Excess and Snobbery," *Independent* (London), 10 Oct. 2002, 18.

13. McCrum, "Self Analysis," 15.

14. Oscar Wilde, *The Picture of Dorian Gray* (London: Penguin, 2000), 137.

15. See pages 6, 7, 63, 132, and 185.

16. For previous variations on this scene see *The Sweet Smell of Psychosis*, 58, and "The Nonce Prize" (*Tough, Tough Boys for Tough, Tough Boys*), 191. In *Dorian* London/Danny appears on pages 184, 185, 197, and 198.

17. Mary Wakefield, profile of Self, *Daily Telegraph* (London), 10 Jan. 2004, 12.

18. Will Self, *Dr Mukti and Other Tales of Woe* (London: Bloomsbury, 2004), 5. Parenthetical references are to this edition.

19. See Stephen Smith, "In the Psychiatrist's Chair," *Observer Review* (London), 19 Jan. 2004, 17; and William Leith, "Welcome to Will's Wild World," *Evening Standard* (London), 19 Jan. 2004, 22.

20. Jonathan Gibbs, "Complex Manoeuvres in a War of the Shrinks," *Independent* (London), 16 Jan. 2004, 22.

21. The project led to an anthology, *Further Up in the Air* (Great Britain: Further A Field, 2003), in which "161" first appeared.

22. Tew, *The Contemporary British Novel*, 118. Readers seeking an introduction to the critical works that examine the contemporary British novel and issues of historicity might wish to also consult Connor, *The English Novel in History;* and Frederick M. Holmes, *The Historical Imagination: Postmodernism and the Treatment of the Past in Contemporary British Fiction* (Victoria, B.C.: University of Victoria, 1997).

23. Will Self, introduction to *Revelation* (Edinburgh: Canongate, 1998), xiv.

24. Ibid., xii–xiii.

25. Self's interview with Leigh, entitled "The Conversation," for the BBC documentary *The Art Zone* is included on the supplementary disc for the film's DVD release (Criterion Collection, 2005).

26. Will Self, introduction to *1982, Janine*, by Alasdair Gray (Edinburgh: Canongate, 2003), xv.

27. Will Self, introduction to *Riddley Walker*, by Russell Hoban (London: Bloomsbury, 2002), vi. This introduction illuminates both Hoban's novel and *The Book of Dave*, discussing elements from the dialect to the postlapsarian condition that Hoban's novel depicts.

Chapter 9: The Republic of Letters

1. Wakefield, profile of Will Self, 12.

2. Hugh Barnes, "Dangers of a Little Self-Knowledge," *Herald* (Glasgow), 12 Mar. 1994, 3.

3. J. G. Ballard, in "Books: The Best of Tomes," *Guardian* (London), 8 Dec. 1995, T20.

4. Will Eaves, "Speeding Offences," *Times Literary Supplement*, 5 Jan. 1996, 32.

5. Self, *Junk Mail*, ix. Parenthetical references are to this edition.

6. See "PsychoGeography #101: Bunny Peculiar," *Independent* (London), 1 Oct. 2005, Features section, 9.

7. Self, *Sore Sites*, 57. Parenthetical references are to this edition.

8. Self, *Feeding Frenzy*, vi. Parenthetical references are to this edition.

9. Abbany, "Self-Service," 17.

10. The article appeared as "On the Road" in the 21 March 1997 issue of the *New Statesman*. The infamous incident occurred on 10 April 1997, and the *Observer* dismissed Self on 16 April.

11. Self, *Feeding Frenzy*, 183.

12. Will Self, foreword to *The End of Everything: Postmodernism and the Vanishing of the Human*, ed. Richard Appignanesi (London: Icon, 2003), vi.

13. Self, introduction to *1982, Janine,* xi.

14. Self, *Feeding Frenzy,* 33–34.

15. Self, *Junk Mail,* 155.

16. Ibid., 157.

17. Ibid., 158.

18. Self, *The Quantity Theory of Insanity,* 8.

19. Woody Allen, *The Complete Prose of Woody Allen* (New York: Wings, 1991), 225.

20. Ibid., 228.

21. Self, *Junk Mail,* 159.

22. Barber, "Self Control," 17.

Bibliography

Works by Will Self

Books

Slump. London: Virgin, 1985.

The Quantity Theory of Insanity. London: Bloomsbury, 1991. New York: Atlantic Monthly / Grove Press, 1994.

Cock & Bull: Twin Novellas. London: Bloomsbury, 1992. New York: Atlantic Monthly / Grove Press, 1993.

My Idea of Fun: A Cautionary Tale. London: Bloomsbury, 1993. New York: Atlantic Monthly / Grove Press, 1994.

Grey Area and Other Stories. London: Bloomsbury, 1994. New York: Atlantic Monthly / Grove Press, 1996.

Junk Mail. London: Bloomsbury, 1995. New York: Black Cat, 2006.

The Sweet Smell of Psychosis. London: Bloomsbury, 1996.

Great Apes. London: Bloomsbury, 1997. New York: Grove, 1997.

Tough, Tough Toys for Tough, Tough Boys. London: Bloomsbury, 1998. New York: Grove, 1998.

Sore Sites. London: Ellipsis, 2000.

How the Dead Live. London: Bloomsbury, 2000. New York: Grove, 2000.

Perfidious Man (with David Gamble). London: Viking, 2000.

Feeding Frenzy. London: Viking, 2001.

Dorian: An Imitation. London: Viking/Penguin, 2003. New York: Grove, 2003.

Dr Mukti and Other Tales of Woe. London: Bloomsbury, 2004.

The Book of Dave. London: Viking/Penguin, 2006; New York: Bloomsbury USA, 2006.

Electronic Reprint Editions

Travels. London: ePenguin, 2002. This e-book contains selections from *Junk Mail* and *Feeding Frenzy* and includes an original preface by Self.

Classifieds. London: ePenguin, 2002. Contains selections from *Junk Mail* and *Feeding Frenzy* and includes an original preface by Self.

Entertainments. London: ePenguin, 2002. Contains selections from *Junk Mail* and *Feeding Frenzy* and includes an original preface by Self.

Sports. London: ePenguin, 2002. Contains selections from *Junk Mail* and *Feeding Frenzy* and includes an original preface by Self.

Nonfiction Contributions to Books and Other Publications

Introduction to *The Redstone Box of Tricks,* edited by Mel Gooding. London: Redstone Press, 1995.

Introduction to *Revelation.* Edinburgh: Canongate, 1998.

"Will Self." In *The Cost of Letters,* edited by Andrew Holgate and Honor Wilson-Fletcher, 126–128. London: Waterstone's, 1998.

Introduction to *Why We Got the Sack from the Museum,* by David Shrigley. London: Redstone Press, 1998.

Introduction to *Novel with Cocaine,* by M. Ageyev. London: Penguin, 1999.

Introduction to *The Unrest-Cure and Other Beastly Tales,* by Saki (H. H. Munro). London: Prion, 2000.

Introduction to *Blue of Noon,* by Georges Bataille. London: Penguin, 2001.

Introduction to *Alice's Adventures in Wonderland,* by Lewis Carroll. London and New York: Bloomsbury, 2001.

Introduction to *Pandora's Handbag: Adventures in the Book World,* by Elizabeth Young. London: Serpent's Tail, 2001.

Introduction to *Antony Gormley: Critical Mass, Still & Field for the British Isles,* edited by Stephen Levinson. London: Tate Gallery, 2001.

Introduction to *Junky,* by William Burroughs. London: Penguin, 2002.

Introduction to *Riddley Walker,* by Russell Hoban. London: Bloomsbury, 2002.

Introduction to *Alasdair Gray: Critical Appreciations and a Bibliography,* edited by Phil Moores. Boston Spa and London: The British Library, 2002.

Liner notes to *Genius: The Best of Warren Zevon,* by Warren Zevon. Elektra/Rhino, 2002.

Introduction to *1982, Janine,* by Alasdair Gray. Edinburgh: Canongate, 2003.

Foreword to *The End of Everything: Postmodernism and the Vanishing of the Human,* edited by Richard Appignanesi. London: Icon, 2003.

"Will Self." In *Un véritable naturalisme littéraire est-il possible ou même souhaitable?,* 23–51. Nantes: Éditions Plains Feux, 2003.

Introduction to *The Psychological Diary, 2005,* edited by Julian Rothenstein and Mel Gooding. London: Redstone, 2004.

"Facing My New Alter Ego." In *spaceBomb: Holograms & Lenticulars, 1984–2004,* 11–12. Great Britain: T.H.I.S. Publications, 2004.

Introduction to *Vera Lutter: Battersea,* by Vera Lutter. New York: Gasgosian Gallery, 2004.

Liner notes to *Before the Poison,* by Marianne Faithfull. Anti, 2005.

Uncollected Short Fiction

"World of Serial." *The Big Issue,* 31 May 1994, 32–34.

"Profit & Lust." *Observer,* 15 October 1995, Life section, 18. Reprinted in *Cybersex,* edited by Richard Glyn Jones, 1–6. London: Raven, 1996; New York: Carrol & Graf, 1996.

"License to Hug." *Esquire* (U.S.), November 1995, 80–88.

"The Human Canapé." *The Idler* 14 (March–April 1996): 10–13.

"There's No Reggae in Orkney." In *Urbasuburba,* by Jock McFadyen. Manchester: Whitworth Art Gallery, 1997.

"In the Union of Facelessness." *New Statesman,* 18 December 1998, 82–86. Reprinted in *Fortune Hotel,* edited by Sarah Champion, 93–109. London: Hamish Hamilton, 1999.

"A Report to the Symposium." In *Incarnate,* by Marc Quinn, 94–99. London: Booth-Clibborn Editions, 1998.

"The Straw That Broke the Camel's Back." In *Nicola Hicks: The Straw that Broke the Camel's Back,* by Nicola Hicks, 3–20. London: Flowers East, 1998.

"20: Will Self." Untitled selection of Self's "Live Novella" from 5 June 2000. In *Fig-1: 50 Projects in 50 Weeks,* edited by Mark Francis, Cristina Colomar, and Christabel Stewart. London: Spafax, 2001.

"A Novella in Several Live Performances." *Independent* (London), 7 June 2000, Review section, 1, 7; 8 June 2000, Review section, 11; 9 June 2000, Review section, 9; 11 June 2000, Review section, 25–26.

"Anything Goes Airlines." In *Vox 'n' Roll: Fiction for the 21st Century,* edited by Richard Thomas, 15–37. London: Serpent's Tail, 2000.

"The Quidnunc." In *Some of the Facts,* by Antony Gormley, edited by Stephen Levinson. St Ives: Tate Publishing, 2001.

"Any Shape, Any Size." *Seventh Quark,* March 2005, 25–30.

Selected Journalism

"Shrinking from Psychiatry." *Times* (London), 15 June 1992, LT4.

"Clearing My Mind over Mater." *Times* (London), 22 October 1992, 19.

"Mad about Motorways." *Times* (London), 25 September 1993, W1.

"Junking the Image." *Guardian* (London), 5 February 1994, 28.

"Drugs and the Law's Pursuit of Virtue." *Times Literary Supplement,* 25 March 1994, 28.

"They Shoot Tourists, Don't They?" *Independent* (London), 27 June 1995, S8.

"Play Things." *Sight and Sound,* November 1995, 34–35.

"The Turner Prize." *New Statesman,* 22 November 1996, 40–41.

"London Calling." *Esquire* (U.S.), December 1996, 42.

"Hell, High Water and Heroin." *New Statesman,* 21 March 1997, 46–47.

"The Royal Academy Is Casting Its Mantle upon Saatchi's Brit Kids." *New Statesman,* 19 September 1997, 38–39.

"Wilde." *New Statesman,* 17 October 1997, 41–42.

"Love and Death in M&S." *New Statesman,* 24 April 1998, 54, 56.

"Artificial Flowers." *Modern Painters,* Summer 1998, 50–51.

"Tracey Ermin, a Slave to Truth." *Independent* (London), 21 February 1999, Features section, 6–7.

"Big Dome." *Granta* 65 (Spring 1999): 115–25.

"The Invisible Woman." *Independent* (London), 21 March 1999, Features section, 4–6.

"Why I Hate Easter." *Independent* (London), 2 April 1999, Features section, 1.

"The Doll Within." Interview with Julie Burchill. *Independent* (London), 25 April 1999, Features section, 4, 6.

"Alone at Last." *Independent* (London), 23 May 1999, Features section, 4–6.

"Come Down from Your Tower, Alison." *Independent* (London), 22 August 1999, Features section, 4, 5.

"Dissatisfaction: The 'World's Greatest Rock & Roll Band'?" *GQ* (U.S.), October 1999, 154–55.

"Doublethink, Doublespeak." *Independent* (London), 3 October 1999, 29.

"End Zone." *GQ* (U.S.), December 1999, 159–60.

"I Danced to a Decadent Drum." *New Statesman,* 31 January 2000, 53–54.

"Wilde Thing." *GQ* (U.S.), April 2000, 140–42.

"The Tate Gets Down." *GQ* (U.S.), September 2000, 340–42.

"Obituary: Elizabeth Young." *Independent* (London), 22 March 2001, S6.

"Living with Dead Time." *New Statesman,* 27 August 2001, 37–38.

"The Year in Absurdistan." *New Statesman,* 17 December 2001, 94–97.

"Ingenious Bubble Wrap." *New Statesman,* 15 July 2002, 48–49.

"The Road as Metaphor of Itself." *New Statesman,* 30 September 2002, 68–70.

"It's a Wild, Wilde World." *Guardian* (London), 5 July 2003, 31.

"The City That Forever Resists the Rational." *New Statesman,* 7 July 2003, 32–33.

"Hostile Climate." *New Statesman,* 31 May 2004, 50–51.

"Schools of Nought." *Zembla,* Summer 2005, 18–19.

Works about Will Self

Articles and Book Sections

Alderson, David. "'Not Everyone Knows Fuck All about Foucault.' *"Textual Practice* 19 (September 2005): 309–21.

Cohen, Olivier. "Self Made Man." In *Un roc de crack gros comme le Ritz,* 41–45. Paris: Éditions Mille et Une Nuits, 1997.

Finney, Brian. "Will Self's Transgressive Fictions." *Postmodern Culture* 11 (May 2001). http://muse.jhu.edu/journals/postmodern_culture/r011/11.3finney.html.

———. "The Sweet Smell of Excess: Will Self, Bataille and Transgression." http://www.csulb.edu/~bhfinney/WillSelf.html.

Golomb, Liorah Anne. "The Fiction of Will Self: Motif, Method and Madness." In *Contemporary British Fiction,* edited by Richard J. Lane, Rod Mengham, and Philip Tew, 74–86. Cambridge: Polity Press, 2003.

Gregson, Ian. "The Caricaturist as Celebrity: Martin Amis and Will Self." In *Character and Satire in Postwar Fiction,* 131–150. New York and London: Continuum, 2006.

Harbord, Janet. "Performing Parts: Gender and Sexuality in Recent Fiction and Theory." *Women: A Cultural Review* 7 (1996): 39–47.

Mallon, Thomas. "A Measure of Self-Esteem." In *In Fact: Essays on Writers and Writing,* 97–102. New York: Pantheon, 2001.

Nelson, Victoria. *The Secret Life of Puppets.* Cambridge, Mass.: Harvard University Press, 2001.

Sender, Katherine. "To Have and to Be: Gender, and the Paradox of Change." *Women and Language* 20 (Spring 1997): 18–23.

Simons, John. "Beyond Human Communities: Self-Identity, Animal Rights and Vegetarianism." *Critical Survey* 8, no. 1 (1996): 49–57.

Smith, Jules. "Will Self." In *Contemporary Writers*. London: British Council, n.d. http://www.contemporarywriters.com/authors/?p=auth88.

Spiegel, Maura. "Will Self." In *British Writers Supplement IV,* edited by George Stade and Sarah Hannah Goldstein, 395–408. New York: Scribner's, 1999.

Vallorani, Nicoletta. "Slipstream London: The City of Apocalypse in Martin Amis and Will Self." *Textus: English Studies in Italy* 14, no. 1 (2001): 163–79.

Selected Interviews and Profiles

Allan, Vicky. "Self Made Man." *Scotland on Sunday,* 28 October 2001, 9.

Barber, Lynn. "Self Control." *Observer* (London), 11 June 2000, Life section, 12–17.

Begley, Adam. "Hot and Cult." *Mirabella,* April 1994, 74–75.

Calkin, Jessamy. "Self Parody." *GQ* (UK), December 1996, 152–54.

Cowley, Jason. "Habit Forming." *Times* (London), 24 June 2000, Metro section, 14–15.

Glover, Gillian. "Will, His Heroin Habit and a Bad Case of Self Abuse." *Scotsman,* 1 May 1997, 15.

Heller, Zoë. "Self Examination." *Vanity Fair,* June 1993, 125–27, 148–51.

Henchman, Anna. "Will Self: An Enfant Terrible Comes of Age." *Publishers Weekly,* 8 September 1997, 52–53.

Kavanagh, Matt. "Self-Examination." *Maisonneuve* 19:40–44.

Lyall, Sarah. "Tale of Recovery from a Bad Boy of Letters." *New York Times*, 16 October 2000, E1.

McCrum, Robert. "Self Analysis." Interview. *Observer Review* (London), 29 September 2002, 15.

O'Connell, Alex. "Tough Boy?" *Times* (London), 18 April 1998, Metro section, 14–15.

Shone, Tom. "The Complete, Unexpurgated Self." *Sunday Times Magazine* (London), 5 September 1993, 39–42.

Taylor, Laurie. "The Luxury of Doubt." Interview. *New Humanist,* September 2003, 12–15.

Index